JAZZ GREATS

Nunc Kelehe

01 · 2·8 · 2670

JAZZ
GREATS

Getting Better with Age

Lowell D. Holmes and
John W. Thomson

Holmes & Meier
New York   London

First published in the United States of America 1986 by
Holmes & Meier Publishers, Inc.
30 Irving Place
New York, N.Y. 10003

Great Britain:
Pindar Road, Hoddesdon
Hertfordshire EN11 0HF England

Library of Congress Cataloging-in-Publication Data

Jazz greats.

1. Jazz musicians—United States—Biography. 2. Aged
musicians—United States—Biography. I. Holmes, Lowell
Don, 1925–   . II. Thomson, John W. (John William)
ML395.J35   1986   785.42′092′ [B]   86-22813
ISBN 0-8419-0750-1

Manufactured in the United States of America

Contents

Introduction

In February 1978 *Mississippi Rag* reviewed a new recording by jazz saxophonist Benny Carter, aged seventy-one, noting that Carter "was playing better than at any time in his life" (1978:13). A year earlier, Carter had been the subject of a feature article in *Down Beat*, which reported that he had recently played "a jazz nitery in New York for the first time in 30 years and was as brilliant as ever" (1977:20). Since Benny Carter has always been something of a hero to me, I went out and bought his new album, *Live at Montreux*. And indeed, I found that Carter's performance on both alto saxophone and trumpet was every bit as good as the reviewers claimed.

About the same time that Carter released his new album, octogenarian blues singer Alberta Hunter returned to regular performing after a thirty-year hiatus. She became one of the hottest attractions in Greenwich Village, and her records were much in demand.

During this period, my own career as a professor of anthropology had led me to become deeply involved in cultural gerontology. Since I had also been moonlighting as a jazz musician most of my life, it was only natural that these examples of jazz musicians who continued to excel in spite of advanced years made me wonder how many other jazz performers were also past retirement age. Leonard Feather's *Encyclopedia of Jazz* (1966) provided the answer. The list of active jazz performers in their senior years was long and impressive: Count Basie (seventy-four), Benny Goodman (sixty-nine), Vic Dickenson (seventy-two), Roy Eldridge (sixty-seven), Lionel Hampton (sixty-five), Earl "Fatha" Hines (seventy-three), Milt Hinton (sixty-eight), Bud Freeman (seventy-two), Red Norvo (seventy), Mary Lou Williams (sixty-eight), Teddy Wilson (sixty-five).

Since a jazz performer's livelihood depends in large measure on his (or her) ability to improvise creatively and capacity for a continuous flow of fresh invention, aging could be a particularly precarious and traumatic experience for jazz musicians—if, that is, old age truly is a time of intellectual and creative decline. It therefore occurred to me that a study of these performers would be an ideal way to examine the relationship between age and creativity, to explore the question whether one's creative powers inevitably decline as one ages, or whether it is possible to maintain and perhaps even continue to develop them, taking advantage of the accumulated experience that is a feature of the aging process.

I approached Dr. John William Thomson, head of Jazz Studies at Wichita State, and asked if he would like to collaborate with me on the project. His response was enthusiastic. So in the summer of 1978 we set out for New York, where we were able to interview six jazz greats: Walter Thomas, Milt Hinton, Mary Lou Williams, Andy Kirk, Eddie Barefield, and Doc Cheatham. The following summer we again conducted interviews, this time in Los Angeles, with Marshal Royal, Johnny Guarnieri, Jess Stacy, Eddie Miller, Howard Rumsey, and Lawrence Brown. (We were particularly interested in sidemen rather than successful bandleaders such as Benny Goodman because we wanted to explore the lives of working musicians who had not gotten rich in the course of their careers.)

One of our first problems was to establish some measure of judging just how accomplished at their art these musicians had managed to remain. Those selected for interviews were thoroughly investigated with respect to their reputation and success as performers within the jazz idiom. A few were no longer playing, but all except one were involved in other creative activities associated with jazz. We attended concerts in which several in our sample performed and took note of the audience response to them; we observed them on the job in nightclubs; and we listened to their recent record releases and read the critics' reviews of these. One musician, Barefield, we chose to interview because everyone we met in New York urged us to "be sure and talk to Eddie Barefield. He is playing better than at any time in his life."

We also recorded the comments of younger musicians who had played with some of these older men or women, and who admired their work. For example, pianist Marian McPartland has said, "Mary Lou [Williams] always believed in what was new and creative; she was a perennial innovator" (L. Feather 1981:19D). And a review in *Mississippi Rag* of a new blues record by Mary Lou Williams in 1979 pointed out that "her familiarity with John Coltrane's music and her recent playing experience with such avant-garde musicians as Cecil Taylor and Zita Carno have led her far afield from the primitive blues forms" (Klee 1979:16).

In 1979 Whitney Balliett wrote in *The New Yorker* that Doc Cheatham's "solos move with the logic and precision of composition, they have the spark and spontaneity of improvisation. . . . Like most of the players of his generation, he is a master of embellished melodic statement" (1979:120). A record review in *Down Beat* in June 1983 of a Doc Cheatham LP, *Black Beauty,* which Cheatham cut with pianist Sammy Price (age seventy-five), gave it a five-star rating, *Down Beat's* highest accolade—which it accords seldom. Describing Doc's performance as "ebullient," "crisp," and "inventive," the reviewer maintained that "Cheatham (surely the only musician to record with both Ma Rainey and the 360° Music Experience) is a model of versatility— creamy smooth one moment, raucous the next, always seamless in permutating a phrase or a single note. Arguably, *Black Beauty* is the year's best new offering of traditional jazz" (Shoemaker 1983:29).

Perhaps the best evidence of the continuing creative vitality of the jazz musicians we interviewed is their extraordinary success in Europe, where some of them make annual concert tours that invariably draw sell-out crowds of thousands. Most appear in jazz festivals at home and abroad, and several are in demand on college campuses to teach, perform, or lecture. The other jazzmen in our sample, too, would make frequent references to "the genius of Johnny Guarnieri" or the "polished, imaginative playing of Doc Cheatham." So there was little doubt that most of our twelve senior-citizen jazz musicians were considered to have maintained an extremely high level of musical accomplishment by the jazz public, by critics, by younger musicians, and by each other.

Our sample includes stars of jazz who helped to establish the art in the 1920s and thirties. From them we sought to learn how they felt about their own creative ability, its relationship to the aging process, how they saw their future in jazz, and the future of jazz in general. We asked them to describe the characteristics of the ideal jazz performance and what they thought of recent developments in jazz and the new jazz stars of the avant-garde. We tried to document the details of their lifestyles, and how they coped with the contingencies of daily life. We also wanted to know what it was like to be getting on in years and still trying to hold one's own in the fickle, competitive world of modern music.

Since these interviews took place, three of the musicians—Mary Lou Williams, Walter "Foots" Thomas, and Johnny Guarnieri—have died. We feel fortunate that we were able to spend a brief time with them. Our debt to all of our interviewees is enormous. From their responses concerning creativity in the later years, their accounts of the adjustments made by elderly artists in the pursuit of their art, and their vast reservoir of experience, we gained invaluable information and insights. Their lives represent indisputable evidence that creative development is not only possible in later life, but can also be more richly productive than ever.

JAZZ GREATS

Left to right: saxophonist Earle Warren (Basie alumnus), Bill Thomson, "Doc" Cheatham, and Lowell Holmes after playing a concert at Wichita State University.

Chapter I
Aging and Creativity

This is a study of twelve jazz musicians past retirement age who, with a single exception, continue to work in some aspect of their profession. It examines their adaptation to the senior years and their continuing growth as creative artists.

Six of these musicians live in New York, and six in Los Angeles. Eleven are men, one is a woman; eight are black, four are white. One was a band leader, and the others were sidemen, although several led their own orchestras on recordings or for short periods on club dates or one-nighters. Most of these people still play, and play as well as ever. Only one has given up musical activity entirely, owing to ill health and disillusionment with the politics of the contemporary music scene—but even he sometimes serves on boards at the local music union hall. Three of them nowadays perform seldom or not at all, but are still active in other areas of the music business. All keep abreast of what is happening in the music world, and all have an encyclopedic knowledge of jazz history. We can expect these twelve interviews, therefore, to shed considerable light on the phenomenon of creativity in the aging.

The Myth

There is a time-honored myth, accepted by the general public and perpetuated by the media, that adults in their later years steadily lose their powers to learn, to produce, and to create, leaving them only the role of bystanders and onlookers of the activities of the young who have taken their place. Most of the substance of this myth arises from a misunderstanding of the nature of senescence (i.e., normal aging), which involves a gradual decline in corporal functions during middle and old age. For example, medical science has documented that between the ages of thirty-five and seventy-five the brain size of the average individual diminishes by 8 percent, nerve conduction velocity slows by 10 percent, cardiac output decreases by 30 percent, and maximum breathing capacity is reduced by 57 percent.

But do these losses in body function necessarily mean that a concomitant decline in intellectual functioning occurs, particularly in the area of divergent or creative thinking? Psychologist Harvey Lehman believes that they do. In his book *Age and Achievement* (1953), Lehman claims that creativity and productivity reach a peak in the thirties and forties, after which they steadily decline. These conclusions are based on his studies of the lifetime productivity of a number of eminent artists, composers, scientists, and scholars.

However, Lehman also believes that the decline in productivity of his sample of artists and scholars is not entirely due to normal degenerative physical factors. It may very well be the result of pathology (physical and mental); adverse social conditions such as marital difficulties or sexual problems, alcoholism, or drug addiction; or a decline in physical vigor, motivation, or resistance to fatigue. Furthermore, in 1966 Wayne Dennis pointed out a major shortcoming of the Lehman study, the fact that most of the people in his sample died fairly young, thereby producing a bias favoring an early peak in creativity. And in a 1963 publication Irving Lorge *et al.* asserted that if longitudinal studies were to be done, they would probably show that aging individuals normally do not experience any decline in their intellectual and creative capacities.

> Age as age probably does little to affect an individual's power to learn and think. His performance may be reduced because of changes in his speed, sensory acuity, or self concept, or shifts in values, motivation, goals and responsibilities which come with aging. Adults learn much less than they might, partly because of the self-underestimations of the power and wisdom, and partly because of their own anxieties that their learning behavior will bring unfavorable criticisms. Failure to keep on learning may affect performance more than power itself. (1963:4)

Much of the research suffers from confusion as to what precisely is being measured. What do we mean, really, by creativity, and what is its relation to productivity? Creativity is a qualitative term, productivity is quantitative. Most highly creative people have tended also to be highly productive, and while quantity may decline somewhat, it often continues at an astonishingly high level far into old age among gifted older artists.

For instance, Duke Ellington's son Mercer (1978) recalled that on his deathbed at seventy-five, the Duke requested that manuscript paper be brought to him in the hospital so he could continue to work on his opera *Queenie Pie*. During the last ten years of his life Ellington composed his second and third *Sacred Concerts*, the *Far East Suite*, the *Timon of Athens Suite*, the *Virgin Islands Suite*, the *Latin American Suite*, the *New Orleans Suite*, the *La Plus Belle Africaine Suite*, the *Murder in the Cathedral* work, the *Goutelas Suite*, the *Togo Brava Suite*, the *Afro-Eurasian Eclipse Suite*, *The River* (for the American Ballet Company), and 137 individual shorter compositions.

But quantitative issues aside, music is a vocation that has often rewarded those who dedicate themselves to it with an exceptionally long life in art. Among classical musicians, for instance, pianist Artur Rubinstein was still playing brilliantly at eighty-nine, Giuseppe Verdi wrote *Falstaff* at eighty, and Pablo Casals, the cellist, confided to a symphony orchestra at a rehearsal when he was seventy-three, "Now we shall improvise. All my life I am working for the right expression of this piece. It is sixty years now, and I have not found it. Perhaps we can find it together."

Societal Values

One of the main obstacles to creativity among the aged in America is the common view that creativity is somehow unbecoming in the old. Men and women who return to college after retirement are often looked upon as peculiar and impractical, if not actually ridiculous. In a society that tends to value education only as professional or vocational training, a person who goes to school solely to learn is considered strange indeed—especially if his or her working life is over.

Margaret Mead has suggested that some of our attitudes about what constitutes appropriate behavior in older people stem from our religious heritage. She maintains that the Balinese, for instance, make no association whatever between age and the ability to learn something new. If someone decides to learn how to carve or paint at the age of seventy, no one is surprised or shocked. Women often take up dancing and men start to play musical instruments in later life. On the other hand, it is not considered odd for a child of six to play in the village orchestra, or even conduct it.

This indifference to age-specific behavior must, however, be considered in its cultural context. The Balinese believe in reincarnation, and therefore what is begun in one lifetime can be continued into the next. In our Judeo-Christian tradition, we have only one life to live, and Mead suggests that "we have put an enormous stress on living out a single individual life, where strength and longevity are related quite differently, and learning is considered to be necessary and appropriate only in youth" (1967:35).

Our notions concerning the limitations of age can become self-fulfilling prophecies for the elderly in America, who either become convinced that they cannot continue learning, growing, and using their imagination, or that developing an interest in such activities is unsuitable to their time of life. It takes a very strong and independent nature to resist the opinions of friends and relatives who believe that an interest in creative work is unseemly in the elderly, and that they should be content to "grow old gracefully"—by which is usually meant slow down and reduce their expectations, both of themselves and of the possibilities of life.

This is a culture-bound attitude, however. In western India, for example, the final stage of life is referred to as the "forest hermit" period. There it is traditional for an artist who has fulfilled his family obligations and done his duty by his caste and society to "turn inward and contemplate the inner light. . . . At this time a man's powers of imagination increase fourfold because he has learned to reach into himself for light, bliss and balance," according to a Westerner who has studied the Brahmin folk painters of western India (Maduro 1974:308). In that society, the elderly are considered to have developed powers inaccessible to the young; they have become more receptive to nuances of intuition, to "conceiving" and to "the unfolding of the self." Released from the material preoccupations of the younger years, they are now free to grow and develop in new psychological and artistic directions.

What Is Creativity?

Most definitions of creativity do not limit it to artistic work, but include a general approach to life which psychologist Abraham Maslow called that of the "self-actualizer." Every creative person, whatever his or her sphere of activity, is characterized by an openness to new experience, a pleasure in discovery. But the late Charlie Mingus, one of the most original and inventive of jazz artists, said about his work that creativity is "more than just being different. Being different isn't necessarily being original. Anybody can play weird; that's easy. What's hard is to be as simple as Bach. What you have to do is know where you're coming from, be able to do what's gone before, but go on from there in your own way. Go where you go, but start from somewhere recognizable" (*Mainliner* 1977:25). He added the very important idea that "love of something sparks creativity."

Mingus's definition is surprisingly similar to that of Julia Child, the "French chef," who also emphasizes that "what is new comes out of what is old. To be truly creative involves taking the art form seriously, really learning the basics. It is a lot of work" (*Mainliner* 1977:31).

Both Mingus and Child stress the birth of the new from the old; no new work, however original, is without roots in the past, in the tradition of the art itself. Being creative in jazz doesn't necessarily mean being avant-garde; creativity is possible within any style. Nor does the fact that a number of our older musicians say firmly that they are making no effort to keep up with modern trends mean that they are no longer playing inventively. They are continuing to elaborate, develop, and expand upon what they have already experienced; for in their youth jazz made them a gift of a lode so rich that one could mine it for a lifetime and never begin to exhaust its possibilities.

Jazz and Creativity

Jazz performance is a particularly appropriate area in which to study aging and creativity, since as an art form it depends so heavily upon improvisation, or impromptu composition. As Charles Nanry says in *The Jazz Text:*

> Improvisation in music means pretty much the same thing it means in other areas of life. It is a synonym for spontaneous creativity, for solving a problem that has not been solved before when working with existing materials. In jazz playing, improvisation usually refers to melodic invention that is created out of conventional melody. (1979:17)

What Nanry is saying is that while jazz playing is not, strictly speaking, composing, the performer in his or her improvisation nevertheless is creating music that has never been heard before in quite this form, taking some standard melody and chord progression as a point of departure. In every jazz solo a new melody is born, which arises from, and is a variation upon, the original melody of the song writer. The hallmark of the talented jazz musician is precisely this ability to invent, in performance, fresh variations upon a set theme, and it is what sets him or her apart from an equally accomplished classical musician.

Nanry continues:

If we think of a melody as a series of notes having some established relationship on a horizontal plane, improvisation involves thinking about the vertical dimension of each note as well, understanding that each note has some known relationship to an infinite series of other single notes. Some of these notes when played together are pleasing to the ear; others are not. The jazz player is enjoined to select some pleasing note or notes other than the ones expected from a knowledge of the horizontal melody. The problem is to select the next note that has a relationship to the note just played as well as a relationship to the original melody. Carried on for a while, this process involves a geometric progression of things to be kept track of: the original melody, the new melody, and the various harmonic and rhythmic relationships between the two. (1979:17)

A tall order for anyone whose senses have been dulled by old age! Whitney Balliett put it a little differently, and more succinctly: Jazz musicians, he says, "are at the mercy of a particularly demanding music. Improvisation, the core of jazz, insists that a performer be an instant and nonrepetitive poet, not simply an assiduous reader of orchestrations, and that he be this lyric creature several hours a night, six nights a week, year in and year out" (1966:240). When we remember that lyric poetry is commonly considered the exclusive province of the young, the continuing lyrical inventiveness of our old master jazz musicians seems almost miraculous.

Role Adaptation and Social Environment

Since creativity could also be said to imply the ability to accept change and deal with its various consequences, charting one's future with skill and imagination, it seemed important to investigate the various ways in which our sample of senior jazz musicians coped with a professional world that tends to honor only youth, an economic world that respects only the fully productive, and a physical world that places a premium on energy and sensory acuteness. We tried to elicit as much information as we could on how our sample handled the problems of the debilitating effects of senescence and the discriminatory restraints that our culture imposes on the elderly, for it seemed likely that the way these problems are dealt with day to day is also a measure of a certain kind of creativity.

If a peaceful life and a reasonably friendly social environment are prerequisites for continuing creativity in later life, one would expect there to be few if any elderly jazz musicians who could maintain a high level of creativity. Playing jazz has never been an easy way to make a living, and it is far more characteristic of jazz performers to die young than live to a ripe old age. Charlie Parker, the saxophonist who helped establish bebop, died at thirty-five; Bix Beiderbecke, whom many believe to be America's greatest white jazz trumpet player, died at twenty-eight; Charlie Christian, Benny Goodman's premier electric guitarist, was dead at twenty-three; Clifford Brown, an extraordinary jazz trumpet player, was killed in an automobile accident at twenty-six. Not to mention the long list of jazz stars who dominated the music scene for a few years, then vanished.

Jazz performers have to travel almost continuously; they suffer from economic insecurity and often abysmal working conditions; they are stigmatized by the association of jazz with crime, vice, and sexual license. Classical musicians often look down on them because jazz was originated by unschooled performers who could not read music. The fact that jazz is usually considered black music means too that racism, never dormant for long in America, is an ever-present threat. Finally, the serious jazz musician is continually plagued by the conflict between the demands of a career as both a creative artist and a commercial entertainer, demands which he or she is often expected to fulfill simultaneously.

There are numerous practical reasons for the pervasive insecurities of jazz musicians: the transience of a life that makes it difficult even to find time and a place to practice to maintain their professional skill, and chronic money worries—very few have become rich; most are not covered by Social Security, and many don't even have health insurance. Survival itself is problematical for most jazz musicians; if they fall ill, they can fall right through the meshes of the social safety net. Then too, they're often at the mercy of club owners who are more likely to be rapacious than generous or even honest.

Jazz musicians feel, understandably, isolated in a society whose view of their art is ambivalent, and they exacerbate this isolation by a kind of self-segregation, through the use of a special vocabulary and an eccentric and conspicuous lifestyle. Jazz musicians characteristically are social outsiders, and they frequently suffer for it.

The musicians in our sample may not be typical of jazz musicians as a group; perhaps they possess certain unusual qualities that have sustained them throughout their careers and may still be helping them adjust to old age. For purposes of comparison, let us look at the study of thirty "top-flight jazz artists" (all men) conducted in 1962 by psychiatrists Cambor, Lisowitz, and Miller.

Most of the musicians in their sample were described as having problems in relating to others (particularly women), and many had experienced some form of emotional maladjustment during late adolescence or early adulthood. This tended to take the form of alcoholism, drug addiction, neurotic depression, marked antisocial behavior, or emotional instability. Jazz playing often served as a compensation for them, especially for their difficulties with interpersonal relations. Music became the focus of their lives, and it was not unusual for them to isolate themselves six or eight hours a day in order to practice. They saw jazz as a means to freedom, and in fact through jazz they were often able to gain a certain public acceptance, while at the same time escaping many of the demands of social conformity—thereby living a prolonged adolescence.

While three-fourths of the musicians in Cambor, Lisowitz, and Miller's sample had achieved what they considered to be a reasonable stability in their lives, their history of emotional problems was unusual, even among artists. If they had made successful adjustments, these were credited, in many cases, to success in the profession, development of warm interpersonal relationships with other jazz musicians, or the establishment of a satisfying heterosexual relationship. Good marriages were important, from both an economic and an emotional standpoint. In most cases the wives seemed to provide dependency gratification, without making heavy emotional demands.

Comparing this sample with the musicians we interviewed, it soon becomes apparent that there are large differences in emotional stability and lifestyle. Both groups display exceptional gifts, but there is little to indicate that our sample includes immature or psychologically dependent people. While most of them are totally committed to their art, it seems never to have served as a psychological crutch. Most of our sample have always been rather conservative, responsible people who had little trouble relating to others and displayed great diligence in the pursuit of their musical careers. Several served as leaders of musical groups or as musical directors of the bands in which they played. Several also have been arrangers and composers, and a number of them taught. Nor were any of them particularly flamboyant in language, dress, or behavior. While they favored jazz for its challenge to inventiveness and spontaneity, all expressed great respect for the classics and believe that every jazz musician should have some classical training. All seem to feel, with Julia Child, that creativity "involves taking the art form seriously, really learning the basics," and that jazz, if played well, involves "a lot of work."

Finally, what does jazz as an idiom mean to these elderly musicians? First of all, good jazz is always challenging. Sidney Bechet contrasted his life in music with the more limited one (as he saw it) of the classical performer, in *Treat It Gentle* (which he wrote at sixty-two):

> They get a whole lot of composers and arrangers to write it all down, just the way the machine is supposed to run—every note of it.

And all that freedom, all that feeling a man's got when he's playing next to you—they take that away . . . All that closeness of speaking to another instrument, to another man—it's gone. All that waiting to get in for your own chance, freeing yourself, all that holding back, not rushing the next man, not bucking him, holding back for the right time to come out, all that pride and spirit—it's gone. They take away your dignity and they take away your heart and after they've done that there's nothing left. (1960:210–211)

Every jazz musician we talked to felt that that feeling of freedom and joy Bechet speaks of so eloquently was what kept him going. Jess Stacy referred to the piano and his style of playing it as his "dope," and Doc Cheatham talks about his "burning desire to play and play." He maintains that "that's why I never drank whiskey. I already had my addiction." Johnny Guarnieri, when asked about retiring, said he couldn't conceive of a musician "who is a real musician not playing any more. . . . Even if you can't go out and perform, you still should do your thing." Mary Lou Williams says that she has "always been happiest when I was playing." And Eddie Barefield insists that "jazz playing is food for the mind. And it's so interesting that you have to practice, because you love to play."

Jazz offers the greatest possible opportunity for self-expression in music. While some of our interviewees find the present music scene depressing, a comedown from the great days, most find salvation in their art, which calls not for "blending with the total sound," as in classical performance, but for imaginative treatment of the musical ingredients in order to produce something that is fresh every moment—new, alive, and unique.

Milt Hinton. Courtesy of Milt Hinton.

Chapter 2
Milt "the Judge" Hinton

Milt Hinton was born in the historically rich town of Vicksburg, Mississippi, in 1910. His father disappeared three months after Milton was born; his mother, a trained musician and piano teacher, was the dominant influence when he was growing up. She was the organist in a little Baptist church in Vicksburg, and Milt recalls that it was his job to keep the instrument supplied with air with a hand pump. Since the Hintons owned one of the few pianos in the community, the choir met there for rehearsals, and Milt remembers a lot of singing around his house on Sunday afternoons, and almost any other time as well.

When Milt was twelve, he and his mother moved to Chicago, where his uncle had gone several years earlier in search of work. Milt's mother bought him a violin and taught him how to read music. But lessons usually ended in a row between parent and child, with his mother complaining, "Why can't you be a nice young man like Nathaniel?" (Nathaniel was the young Nat King Cole, her star pupil.) Eventually, says Hinton, "she was wise enough to send me to this delightful old man, Professor Johnson, who had all kinds of music degrees hanging on his wall. He just fell in love with me, and I with him."

When Hinton was a teenager, in the late 1920s, Chicago offered considerable opportunity for a black violinist. The local theaters all had pit bands, many of which were black, to provide background music for silent movies. But in 1927 Al Jolson made the first "talkie," *The Jazz Singer,* and that was the end of the pit bands. Then in the late twenties Al Capone opened a Cotton Club in Cicero, and Ralph Capone opened a speakeasy on the north side of Chicago, and between these and other clubs in town there was plenty of work for any young black musician who could play jazz. Some of his Phillips High

School classmates who were jazz musicians were making as much as $75 a week, so Hinton decided that it was time to switch to string bass, an instrument he considered more in tune with the jazz scene— although some years later Hinton worked for the very successful Eddie South, known as the Dark Angel of the Violin.

Hinton's mother was certain that nothing good would come of the change of instruments, but in 1930 he landed his first full-time professional job, with the Boyd Atkins Orchestra. This was followed by stints with groups headed by Tiny Parham and Jabbo Smith, one of Chicago's top hot trumpet men. It was during the early thirties too that Hinton first worked with the New Orleans jazzmen, who were universally admired by Windy City musicians. Although a Chicago boy was scarcely in their league, Hinton came to know (and occasionally play with) such people as Louis Armstrong, Freddy Keppard, Guy Kelly, Punch Miller, and Zutty Singleton, a group that dominated the Chicago scene.

In 1932, when Hinton was playing the Savoy Ballroom with the Erskine Tate Band, he was part of a rhythm section that included Teddy Wilson. Then Wilson was summoned to New York by Benny Carter, and when he arrived there he in turn sent for trombonist Keg Johnson, Hinton's best friend. But, laments Hinton, "Nobody sent for me." His chance would come later.

In 1935 he was working the Three Deuces Cafe in Chicago with Zutty Singleton, New Orleans trumpeter Lee Collins, and Art Tatum, when Cab Calloway's band came to town. The Cab's bass player, Al Morgan, had left the band in California, and Keg Johnson, now in the Calloway trombone section, recommended his old friend Milt Hinton as a replacement. Says Hinton:

> Cab came into the club with his coonskin coat and his derby and he did his Hi de Hi de Ho number with the band and broke up the house. He shook hands with everybody and invited Zutty Singleton for a drink. He said, "Zutty, I like your bass player." Zutty said, "You've got him." And that's the way it was. Without anybody saying one word to me, I was traded like you trade baseball players. Cab had hired me until he could get to New York to get another bass player, but I stayed [with] the band sixteen years.

The Calloway years were rich ones for Hinton; the band traveled all over the world, made films in Hollywood, toured America's theater chains, and played extended engagements at famous hotels and night clubs, such as the Cotton Club, and thousands of one-night stands. Many of these one-nighters were in the North, where they traveled by first-class Pullman car. But although the sleeping was posh, the Jim

Crow laws in America in the 1930s and 1940s meant that meals were often hard to come by. Hinton says that their occasional tours through the South were downright dangerous, the band often barely escaping out of town with their lives.

While most of the Calloway sidemen maintain that although a master showman, Cab wasn't much of a musician, the band included some of the greatest jazz stars of the Swing Era. Tenor saxophonist Chu Berry was ranked second only to Coleman Hawkins, and on alto was Hilton Jefferson, whose "Willow Weep for Me" was one of the great Calloway band record triumphs. Cozy Cole played drums, Lamar Wright, Jonah Jones, and Dizzy Gillespie held down trumpet chairs, and Tyree Glenn was trombone soloist and vibraharpist. Walter "Foots" Thomas was the band's musical director. While with Calloway, Milt Hinton distinguished himself with such recorded solo performances as "Pluckin' the Bass" (1939) and "Ebony Silhouette" (1941), and was an important component of one of the better rhythm sections in the business. After leaving the Calloway band in 1951, Hinton enjoyed short stints with Count Basie and Louis Armstrong.

Since the mid-1950s he has worked as a free-lance musician and an instructor in jazz and jazz history at various eastern seaboard universities. As a musician he is offered more work than he can handle and is so busy that he leaves one bass in the downtown Manhattan office he shares with Clark Terry, to save hauling an instrument back and forth on the subway. Hinton has backed up nearly every pop singer and jazz star in the business and has appeared on literally thousands of recordings. His first record was cut in 1930; in 1978 he put together a trio album of his own with Hank Jones and Bobby Rosengarten. That year he also played on the sound track of *The Wiz*, which was conducted by Quincy Jones. Regarding his professional life in recent years, Milt says:

> I consider myself most fortunate for having been in New York most of my adult life, a place where musical flexibility is required. The recording business really began to flourish here in the 1950s—pop, jazz, and classical recordings. Since I had some academic background, I could get into all of it. I played at Birdland or some other club at night, recorded with Andre Kostelanetz or Percy Faith in the mornings, and then did things as part of the CBS studio staff in the afternoon. We also had a neighborhood symphony orchestra that rehearsed on Sundays. All of these things gave me a chance to keep my hand in every facet of the business. I was doing studio work, which required a great deal of reading, jazz work, which required lots of creativity, and the classical work, which required considerable discipline. If a player is in that sort of environment, he can survive quite a bit longer. What helps a musician grow is experience. You have to have a chance to live.

Do you believe you're as good a jazz musician today as you were thirty years ago?

I'm probably a lot more knowledgeable, but I'm also a lot more cautious. You're daring when you're younger. After you get a reputation, or at least become known, you take fewer chances, you try to play it safe. But if you get too cautious, you're in danger of becoming repetitious.

I've got a tape of the first record I made back in 1930, and when I listen to it, I about make a fool of myself laughing at the things I did then. I tried to play things I wouldn't dare try now. Hell, I played the bass upside down once, and the people loved it. I was really playing to the audience in those days.

When it comes to normal performance technique, I'm not too much different than I used to be. I have no physical problems getting around on the bass. Styles have changed a lot, though. Tempos are so much faster, and that makes you play softer. You can't play both loud and fast.

So playing the bass today is very different than it was when you were young?

I think bass playing and bass music has made more progress in the last thirty or forty years than any other instrument. I mean, the scope has expanded. When I was young, Bill Johnson and Pop Foster were doing two-beat and slap, and then came Archie Bleyer with four-beat time. Much of what is happening today for bass fiddle began with Jimmy Blanton, the famous Ellington bassist.

I am very impressed with the present crop of bass players—people like Eddie Gomez, Richard Davis, Ron Carter, and Stanley Clarke. Most of them come by my house from time to time to see "the Judge." But our relationship isn't one where I am teaching them anything; it's more a matter of me getting their chemistry started. I talk about what inspired me as a musician, and what it's possible to achieve. I talk a lot about the future of the bass and the potential of the bassist.

I've always tried to teach discipline and clean living. I think you can be a good player without getting involved in narcotics. I tell them a lot about my life as a jazz musician, and I pick up quite a bit from them, too. What they have that I'd like to develop are things like their dexterity, the way they approach playing, and the way they conceptualize chord formations in the playing of solos. You see, to me the bass is mostly a support instrument. I try to tell young musicians just breaking into the business, "First, you get a job providing rhythm, and then you get a chance to play solos. But nobody's gonna hire you just to play solos; you've got to be able to support."

Have you deliberately tried to change your style during the last ten years or so? Are you trying to keep up with modern ideas?

Very little, I think. I'm using more complex harmonic structures in my playing, with ninths, elevenths, and thirteenths, and more theory, but what I play is pretty much just me. I'm having more success now in slapping bass than I've ever had in my life. The young bass players are discovering me, and they're amazed at my ability to play slap bass. When I started, all bass players played that way, but now I'm about the only guy out in the streets that's really expressing it as a jazz thing. It gets a tremendous response from the audience because it's so visual. Most people have never seen or heard it done.

What about creativity? Is it more difficult to be creative at your age?

I think I'm doing more interesting things now, because of the variety in my background—I'm drawing on a lifetime of playing—and also because I'm listening to what young people are doing. You know, I teach a lot of young people, and sometimes in my classes when I hear what they're doing, I say to myself, "I wish I'd said that," or "I wish I'd thought of that." And later, when I'm playing somewhere, I use some of those things I've heard my students do, and I throw in a few clichés from my own era too. And then sometimes they come to me and say, "How do you do that?" But young bass players can show me a thing or two, when it comes to playing multiple stops and things, that leave me standing flat-footed.

What do you think are the main ingredients in successful jazz performance?

I think experience is very important, but to a large extent your success will depend on your rapport with the audience. When Miles Davis got into that bag where he would turn his back on the audience, it really hurt his reputation. Even though he was one of the greatest jazz record sellers in the business and his performances on record were impeccable, he developed a reputation for not caring about the audiences he played for in clubs. Roy Eldridge, on the other hand, has terrific rapport with audiences. Every time he walks on stage he has a way of making them think, "This guy's really trying to entertain me." I think Louis Armstrong had the same sort of thing, and so does Clark Terry. If you establish the right relationships, the people listening to you think you're playing just for them—whereas in reality it means you can then play what *you* want to play.

What would you like to see happen to jazz in the next ten years?

I would like to see it become truly an American art form—I mean be recognized by most Americans as a great art form. I would like to

see more concert performances, and more television. I keep preach-
ing and praying that young writers or college drama departments will
do a play about Bird or the Duke. I'd like a change in attitude to jazz
in college music departments, too—especially at black schools like
Morgan State, where I sometimes give lectures or clinics. The black
professors seem to be more interested in getting their students to sing
The Desert Song than to do something relevant and meaningful. No
wonder the students reject this and drop out of school. When a guy
like Clark Terry or yours truly comes along, these same music students come right to life, because we come in and play the blues for
them. I think if we ever get the jazz programs established in the
schools, then it will spread to the Broadway shows and the concert
halls and television. You know, I've never seen a good television show
about a jazz personality. A thing called *Magic Horn* was done for Sal
Mineo a while back and that wasn't too bad, but television is really
virgin territory. There is so much jazz history and so many good books
about great jazz personalities to draw from. Imagine what a fantastic
series could be developed about the early jazz days in New Orleans.

Do you play mostly with younger musicians or with people your own age?
I play very little with people my own age. Recently I was playing
Michael's Pub with Joe Venuti, and I said to Joe, "You don't know how
happy I am to play with you because it's the only time when I'm not
the oldest guy in the band." There are a number of us older guys who
are still active, but we're pretty well spread out, so mostly I work with
younger people. I even call guys of fifty "Son."

*Among the young people with whom you come in contact, are you looked
upon as a hero or a has-been?*
I think they look up to me for my experience, and because some
of the young stars they admire seem to respect me. If they see Eddie
Gomez come up and hug me when I walk into a club, if they see
Richard Davis drop everything to come over and say hello, they think
they should look up to me too. But when I'm instructing young
people how I do certain things on bass, I always make the point that
what I do isn't necessarily the best way to do it, it's just easier for me.

*In your experience, do older musicians tend to feel threatened by the
younger ones with respect to who gets the most work?*
I really don't know quite how to answer that. It was like that in the
old days. Around Chicago the older musicians used to threaten to
beat my brains out because I'd get a lot of gigs they wanted. They'd
say, "Send this kid home to his parents where he belongs. I've got a
wife and two kids to feed, and this punk gets the gig." I don't hear that

nowadays. I suppose whether an older musician feels threatened depends on what he's got going for him. Take a guy like Eddie Barefield, who really knows his music. He's such a knowledgeable man, and he's so willing to share what he knows. He never feels threatened. But the ones that are not sure they know what they're talking about seem to think they have something that is too valuable to share.

Tell us something about your professional schedule.

Well, let's run down the next couple of weeks or so. On June 14 I'll be working ten to one and two to five with Quincy Jones, doing the sound track for *The Wiz.* Then the next day at 2 P.M. I leave on Braniff for Chicago to do some concerts with Pearl Bailey at the Palmer House Hotel. I'll be there two days, Friday and Saturday. On Sunday morning at 8:15 I leave Chicago for Washington, D.C., arriving at 12:30, and at 2 P.M. I'll play at the White House in a jazz festival-type event. Monday I have to be back in New York for a prerecording session for the Miss Universe Pageant. On Tuesday at 9 A.M. I'll be in the Regent Studios doing some recording with Elliot Lawrence. At 2 P.M. I'll go back and record again with Quincy Jones. The next day, Wednesday, I'm doing a gig with Zoot Sims at the Stork Club from seven to eleven. Oh yes, I'll be working that morning with Quincy again. Thursday I go to Chicago for another concert, and then I'm off to Dallas and then to Washington, D.C., and then back to the Palmer House in Chicago to work with Pearl Bailey again. On Monday the 26th, Dick Hyman and I are recording some Gershwin things here in New York, and then on Wednesday I'm going to run down to Philadelphia, where I'll be working on a book with a friend of mine for the rest of the week. On July 4 I leave for Nice, France, where I'll be playing for two weeks, and on August 7 I begin working at Disneyland with Hank Jones.

What about slowing down a bit or taking it easy? Do you ever plan to do that?

Well, I imagine that old age is going to force me to do that one of these days. My calendar seems to be very loaded, but these are all things I can do with ease. It's not like the one-night stands with the Cab. I couldn't make it with Maynard Ferguson or Woody Herman these days, but to walk over to a studio and record for a couple of hours is quite relaxing, and to play a festival or a concert with my peers is certainly not all that much of a strain.

With all this performing, do you ever spend any time practicing?

Not *just* practicing. I do more than that. I like to lie in bed after I wake up and plan my day—even if it's just mowing the lawn or corresponding with other musicians (which I do on tape). I don't practice any scales or anything like that, but if I'm working on a particular piece that I'd like to perfect, I put in time on that. For example, if there is some song whose changes I should know but don't, I will look through the book and run through the changes so I can file them in my mind.

As people grow older, a little hearing loss is normal. Does this give you problems?

I don't worry about hearing chords because chords are numbers to me, and I know what they are if I can look and see what the chord should be. My hearing loss is like most people's. I might have to ask you to repeat something that you've said because I have a certain loss of highs and lows, but as far as playing chords, I would have no problems; it's a matter of playing the number I know the chord is structured from. I also think that a bass player can keep playing longer than, say, a saxophone player because they don't expect as much from a bassist, since he is basically playing a support instrument.

What's the most difficult thing about being your age?

I don't have very many friends anymore. Most of the friends I came up with in the business are dead. And I feel sad about that—I think it affects me more than anything else. I guess it's the worst thing about being my age. But the world I live in now is a beautiful one, and I'm so fortunate to have these young people—boys and girls—to work with and show me their love. And they do; they're like my children. But it's not quite the same as having your old friends around. Every now and then I think about Hilton Jefferson, who I spent so many years with in the Calloway band—a great man, and one of the great unsung alto players of all time. And I miss people like Paul Webster and Keg Johnson. None of these musicians ever got the credit they deserved, because Cab was such a great stage personality that all the attention was focused on him.

You know, I have been actively playing jazz for so long that when people see my name on records today they think it has got to be my son. I have had people ask me, "Are you the old Milt Hinton or the new Milt Hinton?" Oh, that's beautiful.

What's the best thing about being your age?

The best thing is being able to do just exactly what I want to do. If a job doesn't appeal to me, I just say, "Thank you very much, but I won't be able to do that date." At my age the most important thing is to be wanted, really wanted. And after all these years, I've even learned to live with the jobs I don't like. I know that many times I've taken a job and after I got there it wasn't to my liking. But I've learned to resign myself; it's only going to last two or three hours. So you purge yourself, and then afterwards you go by Condon's and play it off. Play it off for the rest of the evening. It takes a great deal of discipline and fortitude, but I wouldn't trade my life in music for anything else in the world. It's a beautiful life.

How do you explain your good health and long life?
Heredity. My mother is ninety. I certainly haven't done much of anything to contribute to my chances of living a long time. When I was young I did all the usual things to destroy my life, like any other young musician. I never got into drugs or anything like that, though, although I can remember smoking pot as a kid in Chicago. But I found out early that I can't handle it because it elongates things. It stretches time completely out of kilter, and that was absolutely frightening to me. I found that I couldn't even cross the street. If I saw a car four blocks down the street, I wasn't sure if I could make it across.

Do you think a jazz musician should ever retire?
About a month ago Count Basie and I were talking about that very thing down in New Orleans. Basie is seventy-five, you know. He used to be my neighbor down the street, but he and his wife moved to Freeport in the Bahamas. When he first moved there he had a couple of weeks off, and he said he about went nuts. He walked along the beach a couple of times and sat around his swimming pool a while, but then he didn't know what to do with himself.

I feel the same way. I would just disintegrate if I had to just sit here without listening to and playing music. I would certainly like to play on my own terms, and in my own habitat—I don't expect to go in the Chick Corea band, for example. But as long as I keep feeling I can contribute something in the music world, I want to continue to be involved in it.

What financial problems do older jazz musicians face?
Most musicians have a difficult time putting away money, especially if they're into jazz. We have 35,000 members in Local 802, and about 300 guys get all the work. They make a good living, but that isn't a good average—300 out of 35,000. A few older guys in the business were smart enough to take their money when they were going good and went home with it, but they're the exception. String players who did studio and recording work seem to have been pretty

good at investing, though; you know, guys who started with the Telephone Hour. They used to take their salary in stock, and they're filthy rich now and living in Florida.

To come out ahead in the music business, you had to have a combination of good luck and a good wife to bring the money home to. Some guys goofed and got into narcotics, and some guys invested their money and lost it all in the stock market. When I was young I didn't even know the meaning of money. Even now my wife handles the money because she knows it doesn't mean anything to me. All I want is just a couple of bucks to buy a friend a beer and throw some money in the kitty. I work not because I have to, but because I enjoy it. I have a pension from the American Federation of Musicians, and the size of it depends on how many record dates you've done. So mine is pretty cool. But I can't get Social Security, because I don't qualify for that.

I can't possibly conceive of myself not playing. I would tell any young person this is a beautiful way to make a living. I can't think of a better way to make an honest living—you don't have to beat anybody out of anything. There's a lot of joy in playing good music with good players. There is such variety in music, and all of it's good—that is, if it's played well.

Andy Kirk. Courtesy of *International Musician*.

Chapter 3
Andy Kirk

The Kirk family Bible records that Andrew Dewey Kirk was born on May 28, 1898, but whether in Cincinnati, Ohio, or across the river in Newport, Kentucky, no one seems to know, and on this point the Bible is mute. Andy Kirk's musical career was born in Denver, however, where he studied with an aged German music teacher, Franz Rath, who taught him to play the tuba and the tenor saxophone.

During World War I Kirk and his friends—Fats Wall (an alto saxophone player), Jimmy Lunceford, and Leo Davis (a trumpet player who later was Charlie Parker's music teacher at Lincoln High School in Kansas City)—got to hear jazz when people like Jelly Roll Morton stopped off to play an engagement en route to the West Coast. Denver at that time boasted four excellent dance bands, a black one led by George Morrison, and three white ones. George Morrison's orchestra was so popular that he had trouble fulfilling all his engagements. Andy Kirk and his friends played in this band, as well as occasionally fronting bands that appeared under the Morrison name but did not include regular personnel. The Morrison orchestra, which Kirk describes as "a society orchestra," played engagements all over Colorado, New Mexico, and Wyoming (it was the official Cheyenne Frontier Days band), toured the Pantages Theater circuit in the East and Midwest, and was the house band at the Albany Hotel in Denver for eleven years. In 1920 the group traveled to New York, where they cut records for Columbia, one with a Ted Lewis flip side.

Kirk worked for a number of years intermittently as both a mail carrier and a dance band musician. Then, in 1925, he and his saxophonist friend Fats Wall got an offer to join the Dallas-based Terrence Holder band. Holder, a brilliant jazz trumpeter, had an excellent group, the Clouds of Joy, which included such notables as Earl Bostic and Buddy Tate on reeds. In 1928 domestic problems precipitated a financial scandal, with allegations that Holder had misappropriated band funds. Early in 1929 Holder deserted the band in Oklahoma City, and Andy Kirk, the band's little-known but reliable and talented tuba player, took over as leader. The group played a number of ballroom engagements in Oklahoma for the Northeast Amusement chain and then moved to the Pla-More Ballroom for their first Kansas City engagement. Kansas City, under the Pendergast Machine, was a "jumpin' city" in those days, and Kirk and the Clouds of Joy soon began to draw enthusiastic crowds. A "radio wire" carried nightly broadcasts of the band, and this exposure, which continued well into the 1940s, brought the band new audiences in the Midwest and eventually throughout the country, when late-night listeners all over North America began picking up the Kansas City signal.

In 1931 the Andy Kirk Orchestra landed a very lucrative contract for an engagement at the famous Roseland Ballroom in New York City, and it was then that Kirk came in contact with Glen Gray and members of the Casa Loma Orchestra. Gray offered Kirk forty of the band's arrangements, which he bought and turned over to Mary Lou Williams to tailor to the Clouds of Joy style. The new music not only added polish to the Kirk orchestra, but was instrumental in developing Mary Lou Williams's talents as a composer and arranger.

While the Clouds of Joy are usually thought of as based in Kansas City, the thirties and early forties saw them successfully negotiating a coast-to-coast circuit. The band always had good sidemen, not a few of whom went on to become renowed jazz artists, in particular vocalist Joe Williams, saxophonists Lester Young, Ben Webster, Don Byas, and Charlie Parker, guitarist Floyd Smith (one of the first to use amplification), pianist-arranger-composer Mary Lou Williams, and trumpeters Howard McGee, Fats Navarro, and Shorty Baker. The band could play both ballads and jazz, and they thought of themselves as primarily a dance band. Recordings of a number of originals by Mary Lou Williams—"Froggy Bottom," "Walkin' and Swingin' Cloudy," and "The Lady Who Swings the Band"—sold well to jazz buffs, and a commercial ballad, "Until the Real Thing Comes Along," sung by Pha Terrell, was a hit in 1936. "Hey, Lawdy Momma" and "47th Street Jive" were top-twenties hits in the early 1940s.

The postwar years were hard for the big dance bands, and Clouds of Joy was no exception. As Andy Kirk puts it, "Ballrooms were being converted into bowling alleys, skating rinks, warehouses, and shopping centers. So that was it. Our day was over."

For a time Andy Kirk worked in the real estate business and managed the Hotel Theresa in New York. Once a year he organized a Debutante Ball for blacks, and to make up the orchestra he would contact many of his old band members. He also worked with a small group, the Seven Pieces, on baritone saxophone and with a band of sixteen sidemen, using his Clouds of Joy library of arrangements. When the occasional job materialized, Andy had no shortage of fine musicians to choose from, for he was universally respected in the business as kind, generous, and intelligent.

Today Andy Kirk and his wife, Mary (a fine jazz pianist who still actively teaches music), live in their comfortable old apartment near Sugar Hill, Harlem, an area which has grown increasingly dangerous for elderly people. Besides working at Local 802, Andy is writing an autobiography, *Twenty Years on Wheels*. It's the story of a band that never made it quite as big as another Kansas City group, the Count Basie band, but which is fondly remembered by people who were young in the thirties and forties, dating and dancing in a thousand ballrooms in a thousand towns across the country.

In January 1983, five years after the interview, I had lunch with Andy Kirk in Kansas City. He was eighty-five and mentally sharp as a tack, but moving a bit more slowly than usual because of a recent cancer operation. He was looking forward, however, to many more years of musical activity. As George Simon once remarked about Kirk, "Who said that nice guys finish last?"

Do you feel that you are as good a musician today as you were thirty years ago?

I wouldn't say I was better; in fact, I have never evaluated myself. All I know is that I like music, and I continue to stay active. I just conducted a concert at Carnegie Hall, last Sunday night. It was actually a dance recital, but we did all the accompanying music—including the opening music from *Star Wars*. We played the job with ten musicians. I have been involved in this particular event for twenty-five years straight. I also keep in touch with the music business by working down at Local 802. I have been doing that for ten years now.

Do you still play your horn?

No, I haven't played it in about five years. Not too long ago a fellow down at the union hall, Tommy Mitchell, was after me to begin playing again. He said, "Man, you play that baritone like nobody." So I might just pick it up again one of these days. I do play a little on guitar, and I still write. I recently wrote a tune about Denver, which I'm sending to the Denver Chamber of Commerce. Most of the musicians who have heard the piece think it's pretty good. A friend of mine, a trombone player who works in the orchestra of *The King and I*, asked me for a copy the other day. He wants to do something with it for a singing group. I've also been working with a group of young fellas who call themselves Harlem One More Time. I wrote their theme song for them, and I sometimes rehearse them. I also do a bit of arranging for them.

You know, I never had much time for arranging when I had the Clouds of Joy, but I did help Mary Lou get started arranging. I taught her some of the fundamentals. She already knew in her mind what she wanted to do, but she didn't always know how to voice the arrangements.

Where did you learn all this?

I studied in Denver, Colorado. Everyone who grew up in Denver had the benefit of a good musical education. The music supervisor in the public school system was Wilberforce J. Whiteman, Paul Whiteman's father. Not everyone got the opportunity to learn from him, since he was a supervisor, but he directed a choral group of forty voices that sang for all kinds of civic things, and I sang with that group. Whiteman always carried an A pitch pipe, and we would often sing *a cappella* from that. I also sang in a quintet in our school, and that's where I learned to read music. My mother died when I was three and a half, and I was raised by my aunt. She paid for piano lessons for me for a little while, but I was more interested in playing baseball in those days than practicing, so she finally cut it out.

From working down at the Local 802, you must know a lot of the older musicians who are still active. Do you think they have managed to retain their creativity?

Oh, definitely. In fact, I think a lot of them are even better than they used to be. I've listened to a number of them. There's one trombone player that used to work for me back in the Swing Era who still does a lot of writing and arranging. In order to be successful today he has to be up on what's happening, and he is definitely keeping up with the modern trends. Eddie Barefield is another one. He's a fine musician. The changes that are taking place in music these days don't seem to bother him at all. He still is in demand to tour Europe, to make records, and to work just about all the local jobs he can handle. Right now he's working with a young blind pianist at a restaurant here in Manhattan. The young musicians really admire Eddie. They call him "the Daddy." They look up to people like Eddie and Doc Cheatham because they're thorough musicians, not just showmen but real musicians. Their age doesn't seem to matter.

What makes a good jazz performance?

Well, I think there has to be a theme and a structure to the music. I have to know where you're going. If there's no theme, I'm lost. And there has to be a proper blend of melody and harmonics. A man who knows his horn well can go through a set of chords and come up with a variety of different stories and directions, but there has got to be an overall theme.

What would you like to see happen to jazz in the next ten years?

I don't think that much is going to happen to it in the next few years—there aren't enough people who appreciate it. Of course, the jazz buffs will stay with it as long as it lasts. But it's pretty hard to make a living in jazz unless you're teaching in a college or something like that. The fact that jazz began as a black man's music is part of the problem. In Sweden, Norway, Switzerland, and places like that jazz is very important, but then they don't have the history of racial discrimination that seems to have affected the way jazz has been accepted in this country.

I also think that music has too many names today—jazz, fusion, funk, rock and roll, rhythm and blues. And there are some things— free jazz, for example—that I don't understand. I just don't understand what they're doing. For example, there is this wild pianist, Cecil Taylor, that Mary Lou did a Carnegie Hall concert with not too long ago. I was at that performance, and my general impression was that there was no theme to anything he was playing. Of course, that was the way I was taught, that music has to have a theme and a progression. Since I didn't find anything like that in his music, I didn't know what he was trying to do.

Even in the thirties and forties jazz never was accepted the way it should have been here in the United States. People who came to the dances in those days didn't always know we were playing jazz. They'd say, "Let's get hot," and they'd want to see me do a little dance for them. That's why Cab did so well—he did a little dance for them.

Jazz is also too complicated to really be understood and appreciated. Like I said before, there are too many varieties, and they're all called jazz. It *is* all jazz, but all those names confuse people. Of course, some things they call jazz are mostly noise. But people like Hubert Laws and Clark Terry appeal to me. Hubert is a very musical jazz player, he's not just noise, and Clark is not very far away from me. He's a traditional kind of player. He develops a nice melody; he has a beginning, a middle, and an ending. He's a good soloist.

How has your lifestyle changed since you became sixty-five?

I don't even know when I became sixty-five. In other words, being that old doesn't make a lot of difference. I'm eighty now, and I work with men who are fifty, but I'm just "Andy" to them. My age doesn't make me anything special. I do think that being around younger people all the time is good, though. Howard McGee was nineteen when he came on my band; Fats Navarro was about nineteen or twenty. I understood these kids, and I never tried to play the role of professor and say, "Boy, you got to do this or that." It was like we were all the same age, and that helps keep a fella thinking young.

Some of the people who worked with your band—like Charlie Parker and Fats Navarro—died very young. Have you any idea why you've lived to such a ripe old age?

I think basically it was the food I ate and the air I breathed when I was young. When I was a boy growing up in Denver, we raised our own chickens in the backyard, and we grew our own tomatoes. We didn't use any of these fancy chemicals they use to grow tomatoes today. I also haven't lived a very wild life, going out to ball all night long. That has never appealed to me. I have been married to the same woman for fifty-three years. Sometimes after a job I'd go with the fellas to the jam sessions, but most of the time I'd go home to see how my wife was. When we were working around Kansas City my son was a little fellow, so I never stayed up late making the rounds with the guys. Being a family man with a good wife helped. That, and the fact that I had enough sense not to drink that poison stuff.

What's the worst thing about being your age?

Worrying about living to be a hundred, I guess. I'm not really worried, but I'd like to make it. I'd like to be like Eubie Blake. He's ninety-five, you know. He's a great inspiration because his outlook is so positive. I think his secret is that he never worried about anything. When he worked with Noble Sissle, he let Noble do all his worrying for him.

Do you think most elderly jazz musicians have financial difficulties?

Well, I don't really know because I haven't gone into their personal affairs, but I don't know any who have gone on welfare. I know I'm not on welfare, and I never have been. I work because I enjoy the music business and not because I have to. I like working down at Local 802 because it keeps me in touch. The greatest enjoyment I get is talking to people like you about my life in jazz, and having a chance to talk with the musicians who come in. Howard McGee comes in every chance he gets, and he always has some wisecrack like "I can prove you took that little girl [his wife] away from me." When musicians who played with me come to town, they always come by to see me.

Describe your daily routine.

Well, Tuesdays and Thursdays I'm in the Kingdom Hall; I'm a Jehovah's Witness. I conduct a Bible class. Other days I go to work at the union office. After I get home at night I go to bed pretty early, because I tire more easily now than I used to. I'm on my feet a lot down at Local 802.

A lot of people would be surprised at your spending two days a week teaching Bible classes. Jazz musicians are supposed to be a godless lot.

For Jehovah's Witnesses it's important to be guided by what the Bible says. We're all imperfect. There's not a person in the world—not even the Pope—who doesn't make mistakes. But at least we have a guide in what the Bible says, and I try to live by that guide. I'm not what you would call overly religious about the theological details, but I do believe the Bible is God's word, and I try to run my life accordingly. In regard to religion, I think everybody should do his own thing. As long as you believe in something, it takes a lot of pressure off you. I don't worry about nothing. If something bad is going to happen, it's going to happen, but I'm pretty cautious too. This apartment we live in used to be a luxury house, in a way. We had a doorman twenty-four hours a day, seven elevator operators, and there was a beauty shop on the first floor. But these are different days. Now I'm careful not to be out on the streets at night, because anybody can get mugged around here. We don't worry about it, but we are careful.

Mary Lou Williams. Photo courtesy of Thad W. Sparks, Duke University.

Chapter 4
Mary Lou Williams

Mary Lou Williams has been called "the first lady of jazz," "the woman pianist who plays like a man," "the perennial innovator," and (before her marriage to saxophonist John Williams in 1926) Mary Elfrieda Winn, "the little piano girl." Until her death in 1981 she was in great demand for concerts, record sessions, and lectures on the history of jazz, about which she had much to say. Mary Lou Williams was seventy-one when she died, having been born in Atlanta, Georgia, May 8, 1910. The interview that follows took place three years before her death, on a June evening when she had just returned to her New York apartment after an absence of several days, to discover that burglars had carried off nearly every stick of furniture and every possession of value. The interview was conducted with everyone sitting on straight kitchen chairs, illuminated only by a bare ceiling bulb—even the floor lamps had been stolen.

Mary Lou says that her mother used to sit her on her lap when she played the piano and organ. One day when Mary Lou was about four years old, her fingers got to the keyboard first, and she started to play. Her performance must have been pretty good, she says, because the neighbors were brought in to listen. Her mother gave other children piano lessons, but not Mary Lou. Instead, professional musicians would come to the house to play, and she learned by listening to them. Mary Lou claims never to have had a formal music lesson. She says that she learned by practicing what she'd heard them play, sometimes for ten or twelve hours a day.

Williams began playing with groups of union musicians around Pittsburgh for picnics when she was only about ten years old, and she often sat in with well-known touring bands such as McKinney's Cotton Pickers. While traveling with a road show as a teenager, she visited New York and played with the Duke Ellington band in the Lincoln

Theater pit. In New York she met a number of famous musicians and showpeople, such as Jelly Roll Morton, Segovia, Florence Mills, Flo Ziegfeld, and Bill "Bojangles" Robinson. By the time Mary Lou was fifteen, she was playing in a club where Fats Waller had been appearing, earning a salary of seventy-five dollars a week, a remarkable wage for a teenage piano player in 1925.

At sixteen, Mary Lou married John "Bearcat" Williams, an alto saxophone player whose vaudeville band she had begun playing with in 1925. When John Williams dissolved his group and joined Andy Kirk's band in 1929, Mary Lou went along, sometimes playing specialty numbers for Kirk on a Tom Thumb Piano. In 1931 she replaced Marion Jackson as the regular pianist and began what would prove to be a long and successful career with The Clouds of Joy. Kirk's band was one of the best working out of Kansas City in the early thirties, and much of its superiority was attributable to the talents of Mary Lou Williams, who not only became one of the band's leading instrumentalists but also its top arranger. She also provided the band with such sparkling originals as "Froggy Bottom," "Mary's Idea," "Walkin' and Swingin'," "Close to Five" and "Dunkin' a Doughnut." Mary Lou's increasing fame led to opportunities to write and arrange for some of the top swing bands of the thirties and forties. Benny Goodman's "Roll 'Em" and "Camel Hop" were Williams originals, as was Jimmie Lunceford's "What's Your Story, Morning Glory" and Ellington's "Trumpet No End." The Bob Crosby, Earl Hines, Louis Armstrong, Glen Gray, and Tommy Dorsey bands also performed her work. Although Mary Lou claims that Kansas City during the thirties was a tenor man's town, she had remarkable success on recordings with a group called Mary Lou Williams and Her Kansas City Seven. Many of these sides featured her solo piano work on such originals as "Night Life," "Drag 'Em," "The Pearls," "Swingin for Joy" and "Harmony Blues."

In 1942 Mary Lou Williams left Andy Kirk and his Clouds of Joy, exchanged husband John Williams for husband "Shorty" Baker, and moved to New York. For a while she and Baker fronted their own combo, but then the couple took advantage of an offer to join Duke Ellington's band, he as trumpeter, she as arranger. From 1944 to 1948 she worked at both Cafe Society Uptown and Cafe Society Downtown, mostly as a single but occasionally as part of a trio. It was during this interlude that she wrote her first extended work, the *Zodiac Suite*, a composition in twelve parts, one for each of the astrological signs. This composition was performed initially with her trio on "The Mary Lou Williams Piano Workshop" on New York radio station WNEW, and ultimately in a Town Hall concert with an eighteen-piece band that included strings.

In 1952 Mary Lou Williams left the United States to live in Europe, where she worked principally in France and England. She enjoyed the life of a jazz expatriate for approximately two years, recording for both English and French labels and touring Europe's jazz clubs. Upon returning to America, Williams dropped out as a performer for three years. During this period she converted to Catholicism, hired a young priest as her personal manager, and spent considerable time working for her Bel Canto Foundation, which she organized to help needy musicians. In August 1957 she returned to regular public performance, started teaching jazz performance and jazz history to New York City street kids, and began composing sacred music. In 1962 she performed her "Hymn in Honor of St. Martin de Porres," and while in Rome in 1969 she composed a mass that has come to be known as *Mary Lou's Mass*. In 1975 she performed this composition in an actual liturgy in St. Patrick's Cathedral in New York.

During the 1960s and early seventies Mary Lou was a frequent performer at such New York nightclubs as the Prelude, the Embers, the Cookery, and the Hickory House. Then followed years of appearances at jazz festivals both here and abroad, at major concert halls, and at many colleges. Mary Lou, now in her sixties, was establishing herself as a jazz institution. In 1978 she was offered a full-time teaching position in Jazz Studies at Duke University in Durham, North Carolina. The university assigned her a classroom that seated forty students; 165 showed up (of whom 163 were white).

The creativity of this senior citizen jazz artist is considered exceptional even among her peers. Marian McPartland (who claims Williams served as her childhood role model) says that "Mary Lou always believed in what was new and creative. . . . She kept moving along with the times; that's what I like about her most of all. Once she told me, 'I wrote a tune—it's all about far-out music.' Then she started to giggle. The tune was a takeoff on avant-garde music, and her title for it was 'A Fungus Among Us.'"

While Mary Lou believed in keeping up with the times, she never lost touch with the roots of jazz, and stayed faithful to its essence. Shortly before she died, she told a *Jazz Journal* reporter, "The music today is without the blues feeling—you can play ever so modern, but you must have the blues feeling. Jazz grows like everything else in the world. It changes with time. . . . I've always welcomed the changes and been able to keep up with the new things. But jazz went so far out it lost the beat." And that, she believes, is when "we lost the kids."

Mary Lou Williams died of cancer on May 29, 1981, leaving her entire estate to the Mary Lou Williams Foundation, which she founded a year earlier to enable talented young people to study one-on-one with professional jazz artists. While her genius grew out of a deep tradition based on the blues and spirituals, she knew that she could not live in the past. She focused firmly on the future, and on the young people who would take us there. As Sally Placksin says, in *American Women in Jazz* (1982):

> It's about time that we recognize that of the three (Teddy Wilson, Earl Hines, and Mary Lou), she has been the most creative and aesthetically rigorous in recent years, never resting on her laurels or trading on nostalgia. Like Coleman Hawkins, Williams was one of the very few musicians to have been active, creative, inspired and inspirational pan-generationally.

What have you been doing professionally in the last few years?

Well, for about three years I didn't play at all, and then I began to work with street kids here in New York, teaching them to appreciate jazz, to dance to it and play it. Then one day about seven years ago this Jesuit priest, Father O'Brien, called me from San Francisco, where he was going to school, and said, "You had better come out here and do something about jazz." He and some other priests had some ideas about how I could help them through my talents in jazz, and Father O'Brien asked permission to be my personal manager. I said yes, and he is still handling me.

One of the first things he wanted me to do to help save jazz (as he put it) was to write a jazz mass. I didn't quite know how to start, but I prayed a lot about it and began to feel pretty holy, although I wasn't really. In trying to write that mass I learned something pretty important—that jazz is a very spiritual music. The roots of it came out of the suffering of the black slaves, and it has kept that spiritual feeling right up through Coltrane. There is a reason why not everybody can play jazz—the spiritual feeling has to be there. God did blacks a favor by creating jazz especially for them. God helps people through jazz; people have been healed through it. It has happened to me. I got sick one night, and they wanted to take me to the hospital, but I said, "Don't bother with taking me to the hospital, just let me play." I did, and it healed me—just playing. I'm sure that's done it for others, too.

Has getting on in years been a handicap to your skill and creativity as a pianist?

No. It doesn't matter how old you are. Even if a man or a woman is a hundred years old, they should still keep on playing the music. I think that the older people have let the kids take them for a ride with all this commercial rock and black magic music. There are a lot of kids who are playing rock that can't even play. They shouldn't have picked up an instrument in the first place, because they are not musicians. If they can play just three chords and make noise all night, they can make a fortune these days. But the young have to learn from the old, and not the other way around. When I was young I listened to older people tell me what to do on piano, and now I'm trying to do the same thing in my teaching at Duke University. I have played through a lot of jazz eras—ragtime, Kansas City jazz, and bebop, and I have something to tell these kids about jazz.

You shouldn't stop playing, no matter how old you get. Louis Armstrong never stopped, Duke Ellington never stopped. Anybody that was playing the real strain of jazz, from the thirties to the fifties, should stay out there and play. The music is just too valuable to lose—it was created by God to help poor souls, the downtrodden. About four years ago Dizzy was playing at one of the clubs in town, and he was really great one night. When I got home that night I was so hyped up that I sat up and wrote music until morning. That music was a great inspiration.

When you play with younger musicians, do you feel that they respect you?
Oh yes. I've been a leader of men all my life, and I didn't realize it until recently. Before I went to Europe, practically everybody would ask me for advice. When Charlie Parker got his group together, he said, "I want you to hear it, Lou, before I go out." It's still that way. My students at Duke University come to me for advice. It just doesn't make sense that young people should think that they have nothing to learn from their elders. When I was a kid, people thirty-five or forty were telling me what to do on the piano, and I did it. Down at Duke they look up to me for my experience. Nobody is putting me down because of age. I don't even realize that I am the age I am.

Do you feel that you are a better musician today than you were thirty years ago?
I'm playing better than I've ever played in my life. The older you get, you may not realize it, but the better you are. It takes a long time to become seasoned. I think I am improving creatively. I think you can tell that from my records. The recent stuff is a lot better. Do you know who I did a concert with? Cecil Taylor. The record of the concert is out. Get it, and you'll see. When you're older you *should* play better, because you become more settled. You don't do all those crazy, foolish things. You just play better and with more sense.

Some people say that it is increasingly difficult to be creative as you grow older, that after sixty-five it is all downhill. Do you believe that?

I don't believe that for a minute. You know, my first husband used to kid me about all the expensive shoes I used to buy, saying that I'd better save my money because one day I wouldn't be able to make it as easy. I told him, "If I'm a hundred years old, I'll be playing." And I still believe that. Being black never beat me down, and being old won't either. Age is only a number, and what's important is how you deal with it. I remember talking with Artie Shaw once. I said to him, "Man, you should be out here playing." But he said that his playing days were over. Something discouraged him. He had no faith in himself, I guess; he didn't have the right attitude. I don't care how old you are. It doesn't matter if you're ugly or if you're pretty, if you're old or young. It's what's inside.

Do you still compose?

Most of the writing I am doing now is connected with my job at Duke. I write for a little band down there and try to teach them how to improvise. They can't improvise at all, but they can read like mad. One thing older people can do for the young is give them short cuts. We've been where they're going to have to go.

Have you been incorporating modern concepts into your playing in recent years?

I have always been interested in new ideas. Recently a guy I was recording with out in San Francisco made the comment that I had always been atonal and a bit way out. Andy Kirk used to tell me that I would have to play my piano solos the same every time so that people could remember them. He wanted me to memorize a solo, but I just couldn't do that. Each time I played a solo it was different. And I really tried to do what Andy wanted. A lot of times I'll jam with guys playing what I call "zombie music," and I can do things that almost sound like Cecil Taylor. A lot of people think because you're old, you're corny. But the old-time jazz and the spirituals have a phrasing that is more modern than anything around today.

The bebop music of Charlie Parker has dominated the jazz scene for the last twenty years. Do you see music taking another direction in the near future?

First of all, I am not sure that you should call only Charlie Parker's music bebop. We're not sure who really started bop. When the bebop era started there were about eight original guys playing it; not just Charlie. There was Dizzy, Monk, and Bud Powell, and JJ. When Monk came to Kansas City in the thirties, he was already playing a style like bop. A lot of credit is due Charlie Parker, but there were other jazz giants playing the same thing. I was there when it was created, and I know.

You mentioned earlier the four eras of American jazz strains: spirituals, ragtime, Kansas City jazz, and bebop. Where is jazz going from here?

Unless radio and TV start playing some jazz, it's not going to go anywhere; it's gotta die. But if young people can hear jazz records, they will pick it up and start playing. The problem is that there is only one kind of music played today—rock. This has never happened before with music. A fifth era of jazz is about twenty years past due, but nothing much seems to be happening with it. Even Dizzy came to me and said he was gonna record some rock like Freddie Hubbard is doing. I said, "Don't you do it, man, don't do it. Wait awhile. Don't be impatient." Maybe some little kid, some street kid that I taught here in Harlem will start playing the new-era type of jazz that will lead us. Some people like Ornette Coleman are now playing stuff they call "free music." The only free music is jazz. If I told you what I thought of Ornette Coleman's playing, I'd be afraid to have you print it.

I don't believe that there are any impressive new stars around today. The way the record companies promote some of these kids really makes me angry. They're exploiting the young. Some of the people they are recording have a lot of technique, flashy and all that, but there isn't a single one of them in the same category as people like Ben Webster, Lester Young, Zoot Sims, or Buddy Tate.

A lot of the problem is style. When you hear one of these new young pianists, you've heard them all. McCoy Tyner starts using fourths, and so everybody thinks they have to play a lot of fourths. You didn't ever hear anything different. It used to be that you could recognize an artist by his style. It was a reason to go hear someone play—to listen to his style. You know, when Errol Garner started out he played like Art Tatum, because everyone tried to play like Tatum. But other musicians took Garner aside and said, "Man, if you're going to make it in this business, you've got to create a style of your own." Today the kids don't have the great stars to pattern their playing after. We don't have heros anymore, and we need them. Kids need to listen to great people and *then* move out and create a sound of their own. They always need someone older to lead them first.

How do you develop a style?

I can only tell you how I teach young people to play. First I have them get a feel for the piano, and then if they have some ability and love for playing, I take them back to Fats Waller. And after that I introduce them to Errol Garner and Bud Powell. If some of them want to pick up on McCoy Tyner, I tell them to copy some of his records. They have to copy records, or they'll never be able to improvise. Every jazz giant, including Charlie Parker, started off when they were young copying somebody in order to get going. Somebody like Parker is a creative artist because he is born with something special, some special genius that helps him create a style, and even he started by listening to other people. But most kids coming up, after they learn to copy the records of several of the jazz greats, they have to work to create a style of their own. And that's where they need advice from someone older. They have to have someone telling them if they get too much into one man's style. Playing with creativity and style can't be learned out of a book. What you have to do is show a young musician how to teach himself. When something starts hanging him up, he needs some older musician telling him how to turn it around. That's what I try to do.

I believe that everybody's gifted from birth. God gives everybody a gift, but then they have to work at it. Even with a gift, you still have to learn how to read music. But I don't think anyone ought to have too many lessons. You have to be very careful with teaching. Some of the books that people teach out of can destroy creativity. If you're not careful, you may destroy a person's special gift.

I think a lot of times today piano players are judged mostly by technique. In the old days around Kansas City, we felt everybody was important in one way or another; it wasn't just his technique. One guy might play beautiful chords but couldn't really move on the piano, but we'd listen to him because there was something inspired about his playing. You can learn something from everybody.

You have mentioned several times that jazz was God's gift to the downtrodden people of this world. Are you a religious person?

I became a Catholic several years ago, and that changed me a great deal. I used to bemoan the fact that so many of my friends were dead, like Ben Webster and Bud Powell and Errol Garner, but I found out that religion can bring peace to the soul and dedication to the talent that God has given. Now we don't know if there's a heaven or a hell or what, but I know that certain things are going to happen in life, and you shouldn't be lazy about a challenge. You shouldn't waste the talent that God has sent to you.

How do you respond when people say that you play like a man?

Well, I have been around men piano players all my life, and maybe I picked up something from them. I may play like a man, but I'm feminine. Actually, I patterned my life after a woman. When I was only seven years old my brother-in-law took me to a theater where Lovie Austin was playing. I remember that she was sitting in the orchestra pit with a cigarette, playing the piano with her left hand and writing music for the next act with her right hand. I was really impressed—how could she do that? I decided right then that I would pattern my life after that woman.

Several years ago it was found in a survey of older people that loneliness was their number one problem. Is it for you?

No, not at all. But then, I've always been a loner. I get my inspiration and all my kicks being alone. I have a nephew who comes here and stays with me occasionally, and I love him very much, but I'm happy when he's gone. The reason why I could never stay married was that I am such a loner. When I was working steady with Andy Kirk's band I used to like to leave everybody during the day and drive out and look at the countryside, the lakes or the flowers. My mother said that from the time I was six years old I used to go off like that to be alone. I often pray when I am alone, and I often play music. I used to get very upset to see my friends pass away, but since I became a Catholic, I don't cry that tune any more. Religion is very comforting.

You said that when you were young you wanted to pattern your life after Lovie Austin. Are there any woman pianists today that you admire? How about Marian McPartland?

She's a good player—at least she's getting all the publicity. I'm not prejudiced against anybody from England or a foreign country, even Canada, but how in the world can the English teach jazz playing like McPartland tries to do? I've helped McPartland several times when she was in clubs and she was having trouble with the management; I went and told her what she had to do to stay there. Now Barbara Carroll is white, but she's American and she has real jazz feeling. She could teach jazz. Jazz is American music. The difference isn't so much between black and white, as between American and non-American.

Older musicians often have trouble living on a retirement income. Has that been a problem with you?

I've never been hungry one day of my life, but I have had some hard times. The one who came to my aid when I was out of money and sleeping on the floor was Dizzy Gillespie. I hadn't been working for quite a while and one day I had a lot of money in my account, and where it came from I don't know. I think it was Dizzy that put it there because he bought me a fur coat and had food sent to the house. He did just the kind of thing that welfare is supposed to do. Dizzy really worried about me when I wasn't working. He'd find jobs for me and come and get me to do them, but for a period of about three years I didn't want to play. When you don't work for several years, your royalties go down because you're not in action. Diz would say, "Come on, Lou, let's go," and he'd have Melba Liston come and talk to me. And during that time the priests at the Bel Canto Foundation sent me boxes of stuff. I was just lucky. Maybe praying and reaching God did it; miracles were happening. And since then I've tried to help other people who need it.

Do you still feel you need to practice every day?

I never practice. I practice with my mind. I just visualize my fingers moving. In jazz your mind has to be faster than your fingers. I also hear with my mind as much as with my ears. If I hit only a portion of a chord, my mind provides the notes that are left out. But when you stop playing for a while, your ability to use your mind like that begins to decline. If you are a jazz musician, you have to give it your total concentration.

The jazz greats of the thirties were the greatest because music came first in their lives. They had wives and sometimes children, but the music came ahead of everything else. That's why a lot of people used to say, "Stay away from jazz musicians; they're like gypsies. The music comes first." But that's the way God intended it should be. You have to give your whole heart and soul to the music. You have to keep playing continually or practicing to keep your ear. I'm sure Louis Armstrong never lost his, nor anybody else his age.

Do you take life easier now?

No. I get up between six and eight in the morning, and if I have a pain somewhere I never blame it on old age. My age never enters my mind—I figure I must have just hurt myself somewhere. I have a pretty heavy schedule teaching down at Duke, and then Father Peter has been getting me a bunch of concerts. I go through Washington, D.C., on the bus on the average of twice a week. I don't care about flying. While I am down in North Carolina, I write for the band, work with them on improvising techniques, and I teach jazz history. I do all my work down there in two days, Tuesdays and Thursdays.

I don't believe in taking life easier. I've been around a long time, and I was trained to play almost anything with almost anybody. Over the years I have expanded my horizons and I've experimented. I intend to keep moving as fast as the good Lord will let me. There is only one reason ever to stop or slow down, and that's to take inventory of new sounds and new ideas.

"Doc" Cheatham. Courtesy of Doc Cheatham. Photo by Ronald Eckstein.

Chapter 5
Adolphus "Doc" Cheatham

Doc Cheatham was born in Nashville, Tennessee, in 1905. As a youngster he taught himself to play both saxophone and trumpet, although he admits that he received a few pointers from N. C. Davis, who organized the neighborhood kids into an orchestra to play in the local church. They played mostly sacred music and marches because the congregation wouldn't let them play jazz, but "we'd sneak it in anyway." While Cheatham's father took a dim view of a career in music (he wanted his boy to be a doctor, hence the nickname), Adolphus managed to get experience around Nashville playing for school dances and backing up such blues singers as Clara Smith, Bessie Smith, and Ma Rainey when they played Nashville's Bijou Theater. Doc's first record date was with Ma Rainey, backing her up not on trumpet but on saxophone.

In 1926 Doc Cheatham packed his horns and headed for Chicago, a mecca for jazz musicians at the time. Although the next few years were lean ones, a lot happened. He heard Louis Armstrong play and decided to sell his saxophone and concentrate on trumpet; he taught himself to read music; and he got his first permanent job as a jazz musician, with the Sam Wooding band. They spent the next two years touring Europe. Upon returning to the United States in 1930, Cheatham began a remarkable career as a lead trumpet player in such well-known groups as Marian Hardy's Alabamians, McKinney's Cotton Pickers, Cab Calloway (eight years), and the Benny Carter, Chic Webb, and Teddy Wilson orchestras. After a physical breakdown in 1939 while playing with Cab Calloway (brought about by the strain of too many one-nighters), Cheatham dropped out of music for a while. He then tried his hand at teaching trumpet. One of his students was Marcelino Guerro, who had a very successful Latin band and wanted to learn to play trumpet. After a few lessons Guerro offered Cheat-

45

ham a job with his band. That experience led to jobs with other Latin bands: Prez Prado, Machito, and Vincentico Valdez.

Up to this time Cheatham's reputation had been based primarily on his ability as a lead trumpet player, but he says that playing lead trumpet brings little or no recognition. Although the man playing lead can make or break a band, he gets few chances to play solos.

Things began to change for Cheatham in the late 1960s. His career could have ended then, for big bands that needed lead trumpeters were few and getting fewer. But Benny Goodman hired him to tour Europe with his quintet and sextet, and in 1969 Benny Carter invited him to play in a salute to Louis Armstrong at the Monterey Jazz Festival. Of that performance, Lee Jeske wrote in *Down Beat* (1981), "His one solo on "Struttin' With Some Barbecue" was the beginning of a new phase in the career of Doc Cheatham—from lead trumpeter to name soloist in the course of one chorus" (1981:27). But what kind of soloist can be born at the age of sixty-four? Jeske says:

> Once the thorny label of "lead trumpeter" was removed, Doc Cheatham emerged as one of the sweetest, most elegant trumpet soloists we have—he has a lovely, soft, singing tone and a delightful, parenthetical way of improvising. With his two elbows spread out like wings and his trumpet pointed skyward, Doc Cheatham can solo with the best of them, and he's finally getting his chance. (1981:26)

And Whitney Balliett in *The New Yorker* (1979) described his solos as moving "with logic and precision of composition, yet they have the spark and spontaneity of improvisation . . . Like most players of his generation, he is a master of the embellished melodic statement" (1979:120).

Cheatham's new career has brought not only celebrity but more money than he had ever been able to command before. He was asked to join the prestigious New York Jazz Repertory Company, and he recorded the sound track for Robert Altman's film *Remember My Name* with Alberta Hunter. In the last few years he has played in nearly every jazz festival in Europe and North America, and he has toured Russia, recorded with Jay McShann and with small groups of his own, and was a guest of President Jimmy Carter for a jazz concert on the South Lawn of the White House. Not only has he distinguished himself as a late-blooming jazz trumpet star, but he has also begun to do scat singing. One such offering, "What Can I Say After I Say I'm Sorry," became a hit in France, and standards such as "But Beautiful" and "I Want a Little Girl" are show-stoppers wherever he goes. Although Cheatham won't work late hours anymore, at many spots in and around New York City, such as Wa Chong Restaurant, Crawdaddy, Michael's Pub, The Ginger Man, and Sweet Basil, he is welcome on the bandstand any time he's available.

Cheatham has a host of admirers among jazz musicians and jazz patrons alike. Clark Terry insists, "When I grow up I want to be just like Doc Cheatham." And how does he react to all this attention? He says, "I'm looking forward to living a long time and playing. Playing and living. I have a burning desire to play and play. That's probably why I never drink whiskey. I already have my addiction."

Do you think you are as good a jazz musician today as you were thirty years ago?

Thirty years ago I wasn't playing jazz, at least not solo jazz. I was mostly playing lead trumpet, because there was a shortage of lead trumpet players in New York when I came here in 1928. I only started playing jazz about seven or eight years ago, when I got a chance to go with the Benny Goodman quintet. Benny liked my work, and I stayed with him a year. I've been playing nothing but jazz ever since. After all those years of playing first trumpet, I feel like a bird just let out of a cage. I'm able to play the things I've always wanted to. I think I've always been a jazz player at heart.

I really feel that the longer I play, the better I get. One thing that has helped a lot is that many of the clubs I work in around New York here give me a great deal of freedom. I get to play the kinds of things I like to play, and I get an opportunity to experiment.

Do you feel it is more difficult to be creative as you grow older, or do you believe creativity goes on and on forever?

I think creativity goes on and on, regardless of age. I don't know about forever, but I definitely thinks it goes on—at least it does with me. I don't have any problems. I do find it a bit harder to keep my chops up now that I am older. For instance, now I have to practice every day. When I was young I never had to practice at all. I wouldn't have to warm up, even; I'd just take out my horn and play. But I can't do that anymore. If I don't practice every day, I have trouble. But even now I only practice about fifteen or twenty minutes—just enough to keep my lips soft.

Fortunately, I haven't had any problems with my hearing. The last time I had it tested was about five years ago, and it was perfect then. I sometimes worry about my teeth, but I see a dentist regularly and so far I haven't had much trouble. [Good teeth are an occupational necessity for a trumpet player.] About the only thing I can't do these days is stay out and play until three or four o'clock in the morning.

Has your lifestyle changed as you've grown older?

Absolutely. I break my neck to get home and get in bed every night. I'm a real day person these days. I like to get a good night's sleep. I just won't do that 3 A.M. stuff anymore; it doesn't make sense. There are too many young musicians that will do that. I also like to get up fairly early—seven or eight o'clock. I get up early because I like the early morning air, and I love my big hot breakfast in the morning. Breakfast comes before anything. I won't even go down for the mail before I eat. After I eat, I go out. I walk between ten and twenty miles a day. I walk all the way down to 42nd Street, and then all the way across town and back. I can't just sit around too long. Sometimes when I get home I may relax and listen to a few records, but I don't do too much of that even. I'm not really much of a record collector.

How much do you play in a week?

Well, it depends. I work at a place out in Jersey, Wa Chong Restaurant. They like me out there and I've been there seven years, but only on Saturdays and Sundays. I can take off any time I want if there's something different I want to do. I wouldn't want to work every night. I was at Michael's Pub for three weeks, five days a week, but I wouldn't work at Eddie Condon's or Jimmy Ryan's because of the hours. They stay open until three in the morning, and I don't like that hour. How much I work depends a lot on who calls me, but I turn down a lot of jobs that don't suit me.

Do you travel much?

Not too much, but for the last four years I've been going to Nice for the Jazz Festival. After the festival I sometimes spend four or five days touring in Europe. And a little while back I went to Copenhagen and Sweden for several weeks to do a concert tour. But I won't go on any long tour of one-nighters. That's no good for me; it would wear me out. One of the reasons I left the Cab Calloway band was all that jumping around on buses, not eating properly and not getting enough sleep.

So many jazz musicians have died young; how do you explain your longevity?

I have no idea. It may be heredity. All of my family, in fact most of my ancestors, lived to be eighty or ninety, so that may have something to do with it. I've never been a drinker; I don't drink anything except water and tea, and I even distill my water. This New York water is pretty bad. I used to drink beer or a little wine sometimes, if I couldn't get water. But I never wanted to drink. I get my kicks from playing my horn. I've always been on a health kick. I don't say I'm going to live to be eighty or ninety, but I feel good and I think your state of mind has a lot to do with it.

Do jazz musicians over sixty-five often have financial difficulties?

They can have, but personally I have made more money since I passed sixty-five than I ever made in my life. But then I have to spend more too. With the rising cost of living, they have to pay you more these days. If I'd received today's scale back in the thirties, I'd be a millionaire. I realize it's too late now to think about becoming a rich man, but I get my Social Security every month, and I could live off that. That's why I can take only the kinds of jobs I want to play. Actually I could retire altogether if I wanted to, but I wouldn't. I love to play too much.

Do you think a jazz musician should ever retire?

No, I don't think he should. As long as he has his health, he should keep on playing.

While most jazz musicians insist that they are going to keep playing just as long as they are able, some, like Juan Tizol [composer of Caravan *and* Perdido, *and a long-time regular with Duke Ellington] say they're never going to pick up an instrument again. They say they're retired. Do you think that is typical?*

No, I don't. One thing you have to remember, though, is that while Juan was a great musician, he was never really a jazz player. I was one of the first musicians that played with Juan when he came to this country. He was always a fine player and he suited the Ellington band perfectly, but he never was able to develop into a jazz soloist. He wanted to be a jazz player, though. He was one of the [musically] best educated musicians in Duke's band. He really came up to this country from Puerto Rico to play in the symphony. I think if he had been able to develop into a jazz player, he'd still be playing today.

You started playing even before the swing era, and jazz is certainly very different today. Do you think you are influenced by new styles and young players?

I listen a lot, and I've always liked hearing new things from other players. I think I've changed my style over the last few years. When I was playing back in Chicago, harmonics and technique were different. We are also playing solos faster now. My style has changed a lot, because I've tried to improve. But I play lots of different ways, depending on the job I'm working. I play altogether differently at Jimmy Ryan's on Dixieland night than I do at O'Connor's. It's because the tunes they want to hear are different. Some of the Dixieland tunes are pretty corny and dumb, and it's hard to do the things you'd like to with them.

In addition to your appearances at Jimmy Ryan's on Dixieland night, I know you also have a record on the Classic Jazz label, From Dixie to Swing. *What do you think of Dixieland as a jazz form?*

I never really liked Dixieland, but then Dixieland and New Orleans–style jazz are two different forms altogether. I like to play the New Orleans stuff because of all the beauty in it. I played with Wilbur de Paris in the thirties, and I think at that time he had the greatest New Orleans jazz band in the world. He hated to have anyone refer to his music as Dixieland because he felt that Dixieland was a burlesque of New Orleans music. To him it was music that you played with funny hats, and the trombone players were supposed to do humorous things with their slides. Dixieland bands always had comical publicity pictures, because the emphasis wasn't on music but on comedy; they made a joke out of jazz. We used to call that kind of playing "boom boom, bam bam" music. No, I'm afraid I don't care for the *Original Dixieland One-Step* kind of thing. There is so much beauty in New Orleans music, you don't have to make a joke out of it to sell it. Joe Oliver didn't. Sidney Bechet didn't. Sometimes when I play with Dixie bands I get so bored I feel like putting my horn away and going home.

How do young players respond to your music? Do they look upon you as a hero or a has-been?

I don't know, but most everywhere they seem to accept me and appreciate the things I do. Even teenagers seem enthusiastic. When they come out to hear us, they often rave over what we do.

One of the more controversial avant-garde musicians around these days is Ornette Coleman. Earle Warren [former Basie alto man] says all he is doing is blowing "snakes." How do you feel about his work?

I like what he's doing; yes, I do. But you have to listen to him a good deal; you can't just hear him once. If you play Ornette's records long enough, you'll get something out of it. I could never play the kind of thing he does, but he knows exactly what he is doing; it's just above most people's heads, I think. You know, Coleman was sort of related to me at one time—he was my nephew by marriage. My second wife was his aunt. One time when he was about fourteen he came up from Texas to visit us, and he said he wanted to learn how to play the saxophone. I took him up to see Walter Thomas, and Walter got him a horn and gave him a few lessons.

When I heard his first records many years later, they sounded pretty weird to me, and at first I put him down like everybody else did. But now I feel different. I don't quite understand what he's doing, but I'm trying. I see him every once in a while, and he always asks me when are we going to make a record together. I may even do it some day. It would be a real challenge.

What do you think is going to happen to jazz in the next few years?

I think we may get back to something more like swing style. I see it coming. And I think we'll move back to acoustic, away from electronic music. I don't like all the electronics—I don't think it's pure. The electronics get in the way. I don't think musicians need all the volume and power that you get with electronic gadgets.

I don't know if it's going to happen, but I'd like to see and hear more jazz on television and on the radio. Even here in New York you can't find a station that plays any good jazz. It's seldom that you hear Clark Terry or Dizzy or a really good big band. All I hear is a bunch of saxophone players moaning and groaning. I heard a program last night and got a pain listening to the same thing over and over. I thought to myself, "This could kill a really sick person." All of these saxophone players I hear on a local jazz station sound alike to me. It sounds like the same guy playing all the time. I don't even try to find out who they are. But there are some good people around that I enjoy listening to. Warren Vache is one of the very fine young trumpet players. Of course Ruby Braff is great, and I liked Bobby Hackett. My favorite trumpet player is Clark Terry. I was very fond of Clifford Brown's playing, and you can't help but like Roy Eldridge.

You know, I have always tried to study the work of the musicians I have played with, particularly great trumpet players. When I heard someone really great I tried to learn something from him. And I'm still trying to learn from other people. The more experience you have, the better.

What is the most important ingredient in a good jazz performance?

First you have to like what you're doing. Some people say that they hate some of the tunes they have to play. You should make yourself like whatever you have to play. Louis Armstrong taught me that. He said if you work long enough with any tune, you'll find the beauty in it. Even if it's the worst tune you ever heard, sooner or later you'll find a way to make it sound good.

I have always been open to good advice about how to improve my playing. The trumpet player Tommy Ladnier, for example, taught me always to listen to the bass when you're improvising. If you do that, everything else just automatically falls into place. The most valuable thing I ever learned came from Louis Armstrong. He always said to keep things as trim as possible—not to overdo things, not to waste notes. He never played one more note than was really needed to achieve what he wanted. He also told me about creating pictures in your mind when you improvise. For example, if you play the blues you think about something sad, and if you are playing a love ballad you visualize a pretty girl. If you want a medium-tempo jazz solo to swing, you visualize a buck dancer really laying them down.

All these ideas are great, of course, but what really makes the difference in playing better is playing with great people. Luckily, I've been able to do that. When I was in Chicago playing with Louis Armstrong and some of the other New Orleans people, they used to make a practice of playing every chorus of an improvised solo different—never repeating anything. Some of those guys could really do it too. That was a great education for me, to have to compete with those guys.

I also think a good jazz player should be flexible and versatile. I don't like doing just one kind of thing in music. For example, I don't want to get stuck playing with just one group. You need a wide range of experience. With all the different kinds of bands and all the different people I've played with, I have a lot to look back on and a lot to draw on. It's been a big asset in my playing. It's hard to beat experience. And it's also good to have played all kinds of tunes. The more tunes and their chords you know, the easier it is to function as a good jazz soloist.

Walter "Foots" Thomas. Photo by John W. Thomson.

Chapter 6
Walter "Foots" Thomas

Walter P. Thomas was born in Muskogee, Oklahoma, on February 10, 1907. "Foots" played saxophone in the high school band, whose director, William Mills Dawson, stressed the fundamentals of music theory, insisted on his students mastering their instruments, and above all, emphasized the importance of developing a good tone. Foots gained experience playing for the high school dances. He was always in demand by local orchestras because he could read even the most difficult arrangements. When Foots was nineteen he got a chance to go to work for Fate Marable on Mississippi riverboats working out of St. Louis. Marable bands worked the Streckfus Company ships *Delta Queen, J.S.,* and *Senator* for several years with personnel that included such jazz greats as Louis Armstrong, Baby Dodds, Red Allen, Pops Foster, Johnny St. Cyr, and Johnny Dodds. The twelve-piece band in which Walter Thomas played had Zutty Singleton on drums and Willie Foster (Pops's brother) on banjo. In 1926 and 1927 Foots played with a variety of midwestern bands and even jobbed temporarily (and served as bus driver) for Jelly Roll Morton. In 1927 Jelly Roll's band was playing at a ballroom on 125th Street. He needed an alto sax player who could read well, and he sent for Foots. After several months with Morton, Foots took a job with Joe Steele, a pianist whose band at the Bamboo Inn in Harlem also included Harry Carney, the baritone sax man who would later become an Ellington regular.

In 1929 a group of musicians who called themselves the Missourians (having come originally from St. Louis) were working at Harlem ballrooms the Savoy and Alhambra, and at the famous Cotton Club. Foots joined the band playing tenor and baritone saxophones and some flute, and he did a large share of their arranging. In 1930 Cab Calloway, a singer, entertainer, and master of ceremonies who had worked around New York for years, took over the leadership of the Missourians and with his flamboyant showmanship made them a great success. The band was not only popular but interesting musically as well, and much of their artistry can be credited to the talents of Walter Thomas, who wrote many of the arrangements and who also, as musical director, rehearsed the band. He was considered an oddity by his fellow sidemen, because every time the band was in a town where there was a good saxophone teacher, he would go and take a few lessons. When the other musicians inquired if he was "trying to learn how to play legit," Thomas would reply that all he wanted to do was play the saxophone better. After a thirteen-year association with the Cab's band, he left for a brief stint with Don Redman and a six-month engagement at the Zanzibar in New York with his own band.

In 1944 Thomas and Cozy Cole (another Calloway alumnus) shared a teaching studio suite on West 48th Street. (The author [Holmes] studied saxophone with Thomas at that time.) Thomas's long experience with top-flight orchestras had made him an expert in section playing. His teaching emphasized tonality, attack, breath control, and phrasing. With his solid foundation in music theory and vast knowledge of classical, jazz, and popular music, he was also a great innovator, and may very well be the first music educator ever to attempt to teach improvisation. His course in "ad lib playing," taught both in his studio and as a correspondence course, was unique in 1944, when most jazz musicians believed that improvisation was a gift one was born with, and not something that could be taught. In a foreword to his course material he warned, however, that "for some people it is just as difficult to learn how to improvise or 'ad lib' as it is to learn how to play 'legit.' If you haven't the knowledge of 'ad libbing,' it will require a great deal of time and effort on your part to learn how to do so."

In discussing the approach to improvisation of melodies like "I Dream of Jeannie with the Light Brown Hair" and "Honeysuckle Rose," Thomas stressed chord progressions (intervals and inversions), notation, melodic passages, rhythm (particularly swing phrasing), and the use of repetitions and sequences (defined as "regular successions of similar melodic phrases at different pitches"). During his tenure as a teacher Thomas also worked on 52nd Street with the Walter Thomas All-Stars, which featured Cozy Cole, Emmett Berry, Jonah Jones, and Oscar Pettiford. He also made several recordings with this personnel, including such Walter Thomas originals as "Jumpin' with Judy" and "Blues on the Bayou."

During the late 1940s Thomas got involved in a very different aspect of the music business, personal management. Finding that such a role often degenerated into that of flunky or gofer, he went to work for the Billy Shaw Agency as a booking agent. It was also about this time that Cozy Cole and Walter Thomas shared an interest in a music publishing company.

In 1975 Thomas rejoined Cab Calloway—only for a day, when the Hi De Ho man's band came together for one final time at the Newport-New York jazz festival. At the time of this interview (June 1978), besides booking such top musical attractions as Dizzy Gillespie and Bill Doggett, Thomas was still writing music—a duet book for saxophones and a student exercise book. He had not played for several years, however, largely as a result of a stroke he had suffered in 1975. He said that he would have liked to continue playing and teaching, but his health just did not permit it. He maintained, however, that working as a booker allows him to stay in the business, and in an area with which he is familiar. He believes that he has something special to offer fledgling musical groups because he "knows the country, the problems of being on the road, and how bands should dress and behave."

How do you think you compare in musical ability now to what you were thirty years ago?

Since my stroke a few years ago I haven't been able to play my horns, but in regard to composing, arranging, and writing instructional material for saxophone, I think I am three times better than I was.

How do you explain that?

Well, I have discovered some important things over the years. I have spent a good deal of time trying to break down the structure of chords and trying to understand music as an exact science. I have found that mathematics is fundamental to the understanding of music. I have also found it profitable to put myself in a position of the early music theorists and try to see how they discovered all the principles of music that we take for granted today. Applying math to music came about in a strange way. I flunked math in the fifth grade in Muskogee, but they agreed to pass me if I promised to work extra hard and catch up. The idea of being put back was terrible to me, and I studied so hard that by the end of the semester I was doing so well I didn't even have to take the final examination. Then, when I got to high school and started playing in the band, I kind of put it all together. I came to realize that every scale has a particular number of tones and half tones at fixed points in each of those scales. I began to see that a given note could be a tonic note of one chord but a third of another chord, or a fifth of another. I found that you could always think numerically about music.

What do you think are the basic elements in creative playing?

I think that first of all, a person has to be born with a certain amount of talent. And there has to be desire and discipline too. Regardless of how much talent you have, you still must improve on it. It's all in the Bible, in the story about the guy who got one talent and another who got two and another who got five. The guy with one talent went and buried his, but the guys with two and five used their talents to get more. Chu Berry used to say that if you have an ear and don't use it, you're going to lose it. He thought there should be a thing like the minor and major leagues in music. This would keep people constantly striving to read better and play better so they could make it up to the highest musical league.

Do you think that you have been a creative jazz musician most of your life?

Yes, I think that I have done some things that were a bit out of the ordinary. For example, I was one of the first guys who had enough nerve to play jazz on a flute. Since I was arranging for Cab's band, I could write in jazz flute solos for myself. I also think that I developed some creative ways of using flutes in orchestration. I learned in the early days that flutes and voices go very well together, so I used to write arrangements for singers with flutes playing harmony with the voice or playing a figure to complement the voice. I think I was able to get some beautiful effects that way.

Have your musical ideas been influenced by any of the young performers? Have you incorporated any of their ideas into what you are doing musically?

No, I can't say that I have. Most of my influences go back a long way. I was fortunate enough to play with Jelly Roll Morton, and he influenced me greatly. I think Dixieland had more influence on my style of playing than other varieties of jazz. I haven't done a great deal of changing through the years. You don't have to keep changing to be creative; anyway, I guess we all change over the years without realizing it. Take Coleman Hawkins; he changed with the different styles and approaches, but he never was aware of how much his playing changed over the years.

I learned one thing about creativity from religion. There is a statement in *Science and Health* [a Christian Science publication] that says, "In order to comprehend more you must put into practice what you already know." One day after reading that, I began to experiment with all the different ways you could write four notes. I found that there were ninety-six ways of writing those four notes, using different inversions and different intervals.

One of the problems with modern jazz players today is that usually they don't invest this kind of thought and study on the structure and nature of music. They seem to be more interested in noise. The main concentration is on sound, and they play some terrific sound, but if they were to take those sounds and work them into more meaningful sequences or repetitions of sequences, they would do much better. Continuity of sound is often missing in modern jazz musicians. I'll give you an example of what I mean. If you heard a guy make a speech and he just rambled from one sentence to another, with each sentence having a different unrelated thought, you'd think he was crazy. A lot of modern jazz musicians play like that. Why do people enjoy going to hear Buddy Tate, Doc Cheatham, or Benny Goodman? It's because not only is their sound good, but their solos have a structure, a plan. They sound good for a reason. They play for the listener, and they play something the listener can understand.

Are there any young jazz musicians around today that you particularly like?

I like Donald Byrd and Freddie Hubbard. And I'm crazy about Miles Davis. Miles never did imitate. He has a particular sound, and he is smart. Sometimes he would show up at a gig two days late, and not get docked a cent because he made so much money for the club owner while he was there. He insisted on doing his thing his way, and people seemed to love it. In a way he's a character, but he's a wonderful guy. I have known him for some time, and he's a good little ole guy.

Another top man around today is Dizzy [Gillespie]. When Dizzy joined the Calloway band he was just a young guy and he was playing all this bebop. I said to him one day, "Man, why do you play so many notes?" I'd never heard anybody play like that before. I didn't realize that the man was creating a new style—he and Bird. Bird was a little more melodic in his playing, and Dizzy was exciting. Diz really knows his horn and is well grounded in the blues. He has known all along what he was doing, and he is also an accomplished comedian. I had the privilege of managing him for a year.

Dizzy Gillespie's style seems pretty traditional these days, compared to people like Cecil Taylor, Ornette Coleman, and Marian Brown. What do you think of free jazz?

I don't want to say that free jazz is no good, because at first people thought Diz was no good. But the more he played, the more popular his style got. People finally began to understand and like it. I had a little to do with Ornette Coleman being around today, because I gave him some of his first lessons back when he was about fourteen. I'd rather not comment on the free jazz style, because I don't want to be derogative.

One thing I've learned about music is not to judge something until you have a good understanding of it. I remember there was a symphony performed in Boston once that nearly caused a riot. It was so strange and different that the public and the critics hated it. Twenty years later they performed the same symphony, and it got a twenty-minute standing ovation. Music is something you have to spend a great deal of time listening to. Even though something might sound strange at first, the more you listen the more you may be able to see in it. I think I will have to listen a bit more to Ornette before I make a judgment. I must admit, however, that the fact that he plays a plastic saxophone tends to prejudice me a bit.

Have you ever felt you knew enough about music?

Well, I kept studying even after I had a studio in New York and was teaching saxophone. That was after I had worked as a sideman and musical director with Cab and other bands for about twenty-five years. I had been an arranger for years, but I kept studying theory with a teacher on the same floor as my studio. I'd have a lesson about nine or ten in the morning, before I started my own teaching. The man taught me counterpoint in about three or four weeks. In my opinion you can never learn enough about chords, neighboring tones, and progressions.

I know that much of your time is taken up with booking bands these days. What are you doing musically yourself?

My health doesn't permit me to play saxophone anymore. I also lost my original mouthpiece, and I can't seem to find a replacement. It just disgusts me. I haven't been doing any arranging in recent years either, but I am presently trying to finish a duet book and I am working on an exercise book. The duet book is for saxophone and clarinet, and I am transposing the pieces for use with violins.

What would you like to see happen in the jazz world in the next ten years?

I'd like to see it go entirely pop. By pop, I mean I'd like to see it appeal to the masses—the way rock took over some years ago. The trouble with rock, though, was that it was dominated by young kids. And look at what the young kids did. They came along and decided that noise was all-important. So they bought the biggest amplifiers they could get, and everybody copied everyone else. I think we saw the same lack of perspective thirty-five years ago, when everybody was trying to play the saxophone exactly like Charlie Parker. But they only managed to copy Charlie's riffs. They didn't realize how much he knew about progressions. There was a reason that Bird played the right notes all the time—they had to be played with the right chords in the right sequences. You can't take Charlie's ideas and play them just anywhere. They have to fit in the right places.

I know that you recently turned seventy-one. Has your lifestyle changed in any way in recent years?

It's changed a little bit; I've been doing a little less as I've gotten older. But now I'm trying to get geared up to work more, because I really enjoy this booking business I am into now. I can pretty much set my own schedule. Sometimes I work in the daytime, and sometimes I just go out at night and catch a good act in some club. Last night I went to bed about ten o'clock. I don't stay up late like I used to. At one time I used to drop in some place for a drink, and then go on from place to place most of the night. I have a new appreciation of my home now. Some days I don't come into the office at all; I knock off and play a little golf. These days you don't even have to walk on the golf course, you get a cart and ride. But you do get pretty good exercise.

I don't think much about being seventy-one. I don't believe much in age—it's only a number. Too many people have already disproven the idea that after sixty-five it's all downhill.

Do you believe jazz musicians should ever retire?

Well, if you decide that you want to get into something else, or if you've been able to save a little money for your old age, I suppose there's nothing wrong with retiring and doing what you want to do. Some musicians, like Milt Hinton, are in semiretirement. I guess that means they work when they want to. Now with me, I'm in this other business now—this booking business—and so I feel that I at least am still in the trade. My work is related to music, and I love it. It's a great feeling to take an artist and build him or her into a big attraction.

Have most of the musicians you know been able to provide financially for their old age?

Some of the men out of Cab's band have had some hard times in their old age. Hilton Jefferson wound up working as a messenger on Wall Street before he died. It was sad. After I quit playing I was able to use my experience with bands to get this booking business going, and I have been fairly successful. Sometimes you can pick up the phone and make $50 in five or ten minutes. When I taught saxophone, it took me all day to make that kind of money.

In spite of having had a stroke a few years ago, you seem to be pretty healthy and energetic. To what do you attribute your longevity?

I don't want to sound like a fanatic, but I give a lot of the credit to Christian Science. It really changed my life. When you get into it, you understand that it is the correct way to live. One of the things I've learned is not to pay any attention to time. They tell us not to record birthdays—they only make you feel older. Christian Science has also enhanced my musical abilities, because it taught me where my thoughts come from.

Many of the older jazz musicians we have interviewed have become religious. Is that common, in your experience?

At one time everybody in Calloway's band was a Mason. Now, that isn't a religion, but much of it is based on the Bible. Being a Mason kind of wakes you up to the Bible, so to speak. Jazz musicians need some understanding of life, like everyone else. The model of the perfect life of Jesus Christ helps everyone live better.

What is the best thing about being your age?

One of the best things is undoubtedly that you know how to live and take it easy, you don't have to do a lot of crazy things. And man, we did some crazy things when we were young. Years ago Louis Armstrong educated a lot of the musicians in New York in the use of marijuana. But we learned pretty fast that you never should light up until intermission. The intermission was a half hour long, but if you smoked marijuana it seemed like you had an hour off. And we found that if you smoked during the first part of the evening, the job you were playing seemed twice as long. The bad thing was that many young musicians thought the reason Louis was so great was because he smoked marijuana, and if they did it too they could sound like him. I got over all that nonsense a long time ago; I found that moderation is the key to everything.

And the worst thing?

I guess not being as active as I once was. However, I don't find too many bad things about being seventy-one. I do miss a lot of my old friends who have passed on, though—people like Hilton Jefferson and Tyree Glenn. Tyree and I lived about two blocks from each other. He would invite me over and we'd have a few drinks and talk about old times. I sure miss him.

Eddie Barefield. Courtesy of Eddie Barefield.

Chapter 7
Eddie Barefield

Eddie Barefield was born in 1909 in Sandia, just outside Des Moines, Iowa. His musical career began at the age of twelve, when he found a saxophone under the Christmas tree. Eddie's widowed mother could barely afford the price of the horn, but she made arrangements for Eddie to take lessons from a local bandmaster, although earlier he had failed to take an interest in either the violin or the piano. Every week Eddie was given money for his lesson, but he admits that after the first, in which he learned the chromatic scale, "when my mother gave me the fifty cents I'd leave the horn in the pool hall and go to the movies. But I was practicing every day." What he was practicing (and pretending were his lessons) were solos by Coleman Hawkins and Sidney Bechet, which he was copying off records.

Barefield soon became recognized around Des Moines, and then throughout the Midwest, as a jazz soloist of considerable talent. After working with a number of bands in the area, he soon realized that he would have to learn to read music if he meant to make it his career. In 1927 he got a telegram from Genesee, Illinois, inviting him to join the Virginia Ravens. He jumped at the chance, but after a few nights the leader, Lee Langster, began to realize that Eddie couldn't read a note, although he was very impressive as a soloist. Barefield was immediately given his notice, but he talked with the owners of the band (a Mr. and Mrs. Fath, who thought he was a star attraction) and with Langster, who agreed to teach him to read. Within two weeks he was playing section work with the best of them.

Several months later Barefield found himself in Minneapolis, where he and ten other musicians organized the Ethiopian Symphonians. The band featured Fletcher Henderson arrangements, which they copied off records. The following year Barefield got an offer to play at the Spencer Hotel in Bismarck, North Dakota, and here he first met Lester Young, who was playing alto saxophone in his father's band. The two spent long hours listening to records, particularly those by Frankie Trumbauer, who was a major influence in the development of Lester Young's style and tone. Barefield and Young returned to Minneapolis in 1928, and Barefield spent the next few years working with a number of excellent bands in the Midwest, including those of Eli Rice, Grant Moore, Bennie Moten, Zack Whyte, and McKinney's Cotton Pickers. While playing with these groups Barefield shared the bandstand with such jazz greats as Ben Webster, Count Basie, Vic Dickenson, and Sy Oliver. When he was playing with Bennie Moten in 1931, he says, Ben Webster became "sort of a big brother to me. He used to take me home to enjoy his grandmother's cooking—particularly her pies." (A recent album by Barefield contains a haunting blues number, "For Grandma Webster.")

In 1933 Barefield and Roy Eldridge were jamming after hours in a nightclub in Baltimore. After playing several choruses of "Memories of You" while standing on a chair, Eddie was approached by Cab Calloway, whose band was appearing at the Hippodrome Theater and who asked if he would like to join them.

The Cab's band at this time included such people as Doc Cheatham, Lammar Wright, Walter "Foots" Thomas, and Benny Payne. Recognition of Barefield's extraordinary musical ability came in 1934, when at a recording session the Calloway band had cut three sides and needed a fourth. For some time they had been using a chorus of "Moonglow" as a closing theme, and Cab told Barefield to solo (on alto) on the second of three choruses. That number finished out the record, and the band left for a European tour. When they returned to America they found that the "Moonglow" number had become a hit, and over the years the record has established itself as a Calloway band instrumental classic, along with Chu Berry's "Ghost of a Chance" and Hilton Jefferson's "Willow Weep for Me."

In 1935 Barefield left Calloway and tried his hand at leading his own band. He formed a fourteen-piece group that included Tyree Glenn (trombone), Don Byas (alto and tenor sax), and Lester Young's brother Lee on drums. After a seven-month engagement at New York's Cotton Club and another year's work touring the West Coast, the band folded for lack of proper promotion. Considered outstanding by many, with a few breaks the band might have become one of the most successful of the swing era.

In 1938 Barefield worked as a sideman with Fletcher Henderson and Don Redman. This was followed by brief associations with Calloway, Ella Fitzgerald, and Benny Carter. From 1942 to 1946 Barefield was a staff musician and arranger with the American Broadcasting Company in New York, and in his spare time studied at Juilliard. When World War II ended he and the twenty-four other staff musicians at ABC were let go. The other twenty-four (all white) were rehired shortly afterwards, but not Barefield.

He immediately began working with Sy Oliver, did a few substitute gigs with Duke Ellington, and then settled in as musical director for the play *A Streetcar Named Desire.* (During his two-year tenure with the production he taught saxophone to Anthony Quinn.) The 1950s brought Barefield tours of Europe with Cab Calloway and Sam Price, as well as steady free-lance work with a score of New York bands and combos.

Eddie Barefield has been teaching arranging, saxophone, clarinet, flute, and piccolo for over thirty years. He still works regularly with New York jazz groups, travels to Europe almost annually for jazz festivals, and is a regular in the band that plays for the Ice Capades and the Ringling Brothers Circus when they play Madison Square Garden.

Eddie Barefield is married to Connie Harris, a modern dancer who has appeared in over thirty-five Hollywood films. He practices several hours a day, maintains a rigorous exercise program of walking, golfing, and weight-lifting, and still manages to get together a group now and then for a recording session. On a recent album, *The Indestructible Eddie Barefield* (Famous Door Records), he performs a half-dozen original compositions with a hand-picked rhythm section (including Milt Hinton) and two of the jazz world's highly touted young trumpet players, Jon Faddis and Warren Vache.

The night before we interviewed Eddie Barefield, we dropped in to hear him play in a lounge up near Central Park. He was playing tenor (his preference in recent years) with a group made up of Brooks Kerr, a young blind pianist, and old-timer Sonny Greer on drums. Everyone we had interviewed previously had urged us to be sure and talk to Eddie Barefield, because "Eddie is playing better than ever these days." They were right.

Do you think that you are as good a musician today as you were thirty years ago?

I think I'm a better musician today. At least, I'm trying to be a better player. I can't remember exactly how I played in the early days, though. I know that when I was young it was a lot easier, I was a lot quicker and more technically proficient on my horn. It didn't seem to take quite as much effort then—but now I am a lot more knowledgeable about music, and all those years of experience as a jazz player in so many great bands have made an enormous difference in the quality of my playing.

Have you consciously changed your style of playing to keep up with modern trends?

I think that happens automatically. As you work with and listen to players with new ideas, it affects the way you play without your realizing it. I know I used to kid Coleman Hawkins about some of the things he used to do on solos back in the 1920s—like slap-tone solos and ricky-ticky ideas. I once played him some of his early recordings, and he wouldn't even admit that it was him playing. One thing I don't like to see is someone trying to go back in time. Bob Wilbur, for example, idolizes Sidney Bechet, and when he started playing all he wanted to do was sound exactly like Bechet. Fortunately he has matured as a musician and has moved beyond Bechet imitation and developed into an outstanding and versatile saxophone and clarinet player.

What have been the main musical influences on you?

One of the greatest influences on me was a guy who in a way was my protégé, Don Byas. He was playing alto in my band in California, and I made him switch to tenor. He had never played tenor before, and he resented the fact that I wouldn't let him play alto, but I think he became the greatest tenor player who ever lived. By listening to his records I'm trying to learn from him what he said I taught him. In my opinion, he had everything. He was fast, he could play ballads, and he had a beautiful mind and a great ear.

Do you still practice every day?

I practice as much as I can. I mean, I can't wait to get home to practice. I drive my wife crazy. I only practice on tenor these days. I play flute, piccolo, and clarinet, but I don't touch them much unless it's required on a job. If I practice, my chops stay pretty hot, but when I don't practice, they don't. If I lay off three or four days, I know it. I keep practicing because there are a lot of things I want to do on the horn that I'm not able to do yet.

Do you do any composing? Do you think age affects a musician's ability to compose?

Well, I do writing and composing for my own groups and my own records, but I don't do it for others. Composing has nothing to do with age, it's something that is second nature. All jazz players are composers. I mean, if you're playing jazz you're composing all the time. So sitting down to write something is never any problem.

Do you do any teaching now?
Yes, I teach some, but you really couldn't call me a saxophone teacher these days. I'm down to three students. I have discarded a considerable number of students because I find that only about one person in fifteen really wants to play and is willing to work at it. I had about forty students at one time, but I found it was a waste of time. Mostly it took me away from my own playing and practicing. Now I only have three really serious people, who work on their own and give me a call when they need my help on something.

When you work, do you play mostly with people your own age?
No. I play with everybody. The guy I'm playing with tonight is younger. There are not too many old guys around to play with, and those that are doing good are very busy. But I keep pretty busy, because I have to make a living. So I play different club dates, and play with different bands. I also play at Madison Square Garden. I just finished three months at the Garden with the circus. The shows there are three hours long, with three shows on Saturday. It's very tiring, but after about a week you get used to it.

I don't see too many really young musicians. Most of the people I work with are established people. I don't get a chance to work with many young fellows unless they have the same contacts I have.

Do you get the impression that people think you're a jazz hero, or do you feel like a "has been"?
Well, I'm a pretty sociable guy you know, so I haven't had that feeling. I know that there is a certain group of guys that don't call guys like me for jobs. But that's their bag, and if they want to do that it's O.K.

Do you have any problems with playing that are connected with your age?
I have a bit of a hearing problem. My wife says I can't hear because I always turn the television up, but it hasn't affected my playing. The hearing loss is probably caused by sitting in front of brass sections all my life.

What is your reaction to some of the more recent jazz artists, like Ornette Coleman?
I don't know much about Coleman's ability, but from what I have heard on records, I don't think it takes any musical knowledge at all to

do what he's doing. He does nothing for me—but then I don't listen to
music like the average person does. I listen for the harmonic content
of the music, and whether the guy plays with soul. Just playing notes
isn't anything unless there's some meaning to the harmonic structure.
Although harmonic structures have gotten a little more complex in
the last ten or fifteen years, they haven't gotten out of context with the
music. People like Bird and Art Tatum—people way ahead of their
time—modified and improvised chord progressions, but they didn't
make them outlandish.

*What do you think of some of the other modern saxophone players, like Lee
Konitz, Paul Desmond, and Phil Woods?*

Lee's a good player, but I never liked Desmond much. He always
sounded like his horn had a cold. Woods is the biggest, but the
greatest alto player of recent years was Cannonball Adderly. Cannonball played a saxophone like it was supposed to be played. He was a
hybrid between Benny Carter and Charlie Parker. He played all of
the Bird's stuff, but he had more of a Carter feeling for it. He had a
great ear. I think the ear is something that you can't get away from. If
you have an ear and you follow it, you can't go wrong. Take Louis
Armstrong. He never had any knowledge of music. But his ear was so
good that he never played a wrong note. Sidney Bechet was another
one like that, and also Lester Young. Lester had no knowledge of
music. He just had a good ear—he listened to things and his ear could
pick them up. Lester didn't know one chord from another.

What do you think is the most important thing in playing good jazz?

Well, it's a combination of things. First, you've got to have an ear
for music, an analytic ear. Then you have to learn your harmony, and
you must practice to build your technique, and then you have to have
somebody really outstanding to listen to. I was fortunate because I
had an opportunity to play with people like Art Tatum, Benny Carter,
and Coleman Hawkins. Since there's no opportunity today to play
with these guys, a good thing to do is just listen. But a lot of kids don't
know who to listen to. If you've got the ear and the talent, you'll get it.
A great jazz soloist with an outstanding ear is Roy Eldridge. Playing
great jazz is just a natural thing to Roy. Dizzy Gillespie also has a great
ear, but he has more—he also plays with the mind. With the combination of the two, the mind and the ear, there's no limit to what you can
do.

Another important thing in playing good jazz is getting out and
doing it. From the very beginning, I was a jammer. I used to go out
every night after work and find someplace to jam. That's where I got a

lot of my jazz-playing ability from—just jamming every night. I had to do that because on most of the jobs I was just playing lead alto and not getting much chance to solo and improvise.

What do you think is going to happen to jazz in the next ten years?

Nothing. Because jazz is beyond the comprehension of the average person. That's the reason big bands can't make it—it's too much for people to listen to. Remember John Kirby's little group? That was a great band for people to listen to, because they only had to hear three-part harmony. But when the average person has to listen to a saxophone section, a trumpet section, a trombone section, and a rhythm section, it becomes confusing. The musicians today are great, but somebody's got to support the music business.

What would you like to see happen to jazz in the next ten years?

I'd love to see somebody promote it. People would buy it—all it needs is promotion. Because people don't know the difference anyway. I don't mean to put the public down, but they're not very intelligent about music. In Europe they are a lot more knowledgeable about jazz. They sit down in their clubs and they listen to it. This whole country is a bunch of hillbillies. When it comes to appreciating music in this country, all anybody wants to hear is something simple like country and western or rock and roll.

Country and western is strictly IV I V harmony, and the rock and roll they play today is all one chord, or maybe two or three; the biggest thing is rhythm.

People in this country don't know the difference between good music and bad. When people listen to jazz, they ask you, "Is he good?" or "Is that good?" They don't know the difference because they have only had one kind of music to listen to. Today, if you have a group that packs them in in one joint, then every other joint in town tries to get a group that sounds exactly like them. Everybody follows the next guy, and nobody seems to have any ideas of his own. We need a little education in this country about what is good jazz. Here in New York we have the Duke Ellington Jazz Club, where people come together to listen to and analyze records. These people aren't musicians, by and large, but you don't have to be a musician to learn about what is good in jazz. You don't find this kind of thing happening much across the country, though. And nobody is promoting jazz today.

When I played with Cab Calloway and Jay McShann, they would advertise our appearance for six or seven months beforehand. When you drove down the highway you would see billboards that read "Cab Calloway—appearing at the Crystal Ballroom on November the 7th."

And this made people come out. But today when you go into a town, you don't know where anybody's playing. Roy Eldridge has been at Ryan's here in New York for about five years, and nobody knows it; they don't advertise.

Has your lifestyle changed as you've grown older?

I don't travel as much as I did, and I used to love it. But traveling conditions are horrid now, especially by plane. You spend most of your time in airports. You never get to see anything when you travel nowadays. They put you in a motel outside of town. In the old days you'd stay in a hotel someplace right in the heart of things, and you played the job in town. You got to meet people, and they were sociable. Today when you go to play a concert, before you get your horn packed up everybody's gone.

Since I've gotten older I've become a day person. I'm only out at night when I'm working. When I have a free night I'm in bed at nine o'clock. But I don't sleep like other people, I sleep in spurts of an hour or so. I stay in bed for eight or nine hours, but I don't sleep all the time. I've learned to relax without sleeping. I lie in bed and think about chord changes and what I am going to practice tomorrow.

How do you account for your long life and good health in a profession in which so many people have died young?

I'm a health addict. I've exercised all my life, and I take vitamins. I run, and I lift weights. I used to play baseball. When I was with Cab Calloway we had a hardball team, and I also used to play a lot of softball around New York. I was a boxer too. And then I'm a real hypochondriac. The least little thing, and I start to holler. I have a bunch of oriental teas that I drink too. At my age you can't afford to take chances with your health, you can't afford to lose anything. My wife laughs at me a lot. She's the same age that I am, but I don't have her stamina, although everyone thinks that I'm in good condition. All of them call me the strong man of music.

Do you drink?

No. I used to; I drank, like everybody else. But I don't even drink beer now, and I don't smoke either.

Do you think a jazz player should ever retire?

No. I think it's a way of life. It's like praying or eating. When you're into that sort of thing, you can't stop. Jazz playing is food for the mind. And it's so interesting, you have to practice because you love to play. I just love to play the tenor. All I ask is the ideal situation now and then—a good piano player, a good drummer, and a good bass player. And I get it once in a while.

Do musicians your age who have spent a lifetime playing jazz tend to have financial problems, or have they usually been able to set something aside for their later years?

I imagine they do have financial problems. I know I don't have any money, but I was able to buy a house, and we're comfortable there. I have sufficient income to keep it going. I have a little car, and my bills are paid. I could never make it on Social Security. I have to keep working. I always say a man is rich if he feels good. I guess I'll have to settle for that kind of wealth.

Let's say that you had managed to get rich during your playing days. What would you do with your money?

I'd have a band, and I'd have me a club. Right now if I fell into some money, say a million dollars, I'd open a joint and have me about six or seven pieces in there, or maybe a quartet. And every once in a while we'd go on the road and I'd bring somebody else in to play. There wouldn't be nothing but jazz played there.

We've noticed that many of the old-time jazz people are quite religious. Are you religious?

I don't belong to a church, but I believe in God. My mother was a Methodist and my father a Baptist. I had to go to church and Sunday school every Sunday, or else I couldn't do anything else I wanted to do. I used to listen to what the preachers said, and there were a lot of things I just couldn't go along with. So I started studying different religions on my own. And I talked to a lot of preachers because I wanted to find God. Then about thirty years ago I discovered Yoga and found a whole philosophy of life. I became a Yogist—but then everyone is a Yogist, they just don't know it. But I got on the Path and started studying the philosophy. I'm not talking about standing on your head and all that. I'm talking about the evolution of the spirit.

What are the best and worst things about being over sixty-five?

There is nothing good about being over sixty-five. I wish I was in my twenties again. Not that I liked what was happening to me then, but I wish I had the stamina I had then. And the worst thing about being over sixty-five is being over sixty-five. When you get up to where I am in life, there are only a few really important things left—like a pretty girl and my horn.

Johnny Guarnieri. Courtesy of Mrs. Jeanne Guarnieri.

Chapter 8
Johnny Guarnieri

Johnny Guarnieri has been described as a musicologist, a genius, and a "superstride" piano player. His name alone would suggest that his remarkable musical talent was inherited; he was born into the family of famous violin makers in New York City on March 23, 1917. His father was a violinist as well as a violin maker, and his brother is a bassist. He began classical piano study at the age of ten, and before long he was accompanying his father.

He soon began to experience the lure of popular music, especially that of such composers as Gershwin, Porter, and Kern. As a teenager Guarnieri began hanging out at the Brill Building, a meeting place for songwriters, publishers, and musicians. Here he got to know such jazz stars as Fats Waller, James P. Johnson, and Willie (the Lion) Smith. While playing piano in a publisher's studio one day, Guarnieri was noticed by George Hill and Dolly Dawn. They liked his style and offered him a job with the George Hill band, whose rhythm section already included Doc Goldberg (later a Glenn Miller sideman) on bass, Nick Fatool on drums, and Tony Mottola on guitar. Guarnieri played with Hill's band at the Taft Hotel from 1937 until 1939, when he realized the ambition of his life—to play with Benny Goodman. "When I joined Benny Goodman it was a fulfillment of a dream," he says, but while he "enjoyed every minute of it," the job was no bed of roses. He recalls:

> When I first joined Benny, he called me "Fletcher" for three months before he could remember my name. And he told me I was the worst piano player he'd had since Frankie Froeba. He didn't like my so-called "imitating" other pianists . . . Both Lionel Hampton and Charlie Christian would tell me, "Don't let Benny scare you, you're a *piano player*, Johnny—and you *swing*." As a matter of fact, Lionel and Charlie were the only two guys in the band who would talk to me

when I joined. All the other guys were "big shots" and I wasn't. (Shapiro and Hentoff 1955:321)

Guarnieri stayed with the Goodman band only about six months, until the summer of 1940, but during that period he made a number of records both with the full band and with sextet and septet groups within it, including the now-famous cutting of "Solo Flight," which featured Charlie Christian on electric guitar. After leaving Goodman, Johnny moved to the Artie Shaw band, where he again became an important part of a band within a band, in this case the Gramercy Five, in which Guarnieri played harpsichord. Some of the records cut during this period—"Special Delivery Stomp," "Summit Ridge Drive," and "My Blue Heaven"—were among Shaw's biggest hits. In 1941 Guarnieri moved back to Goodman for another six months, then back again to Shaw for an even briefer period. After the temperamental Goodman and Shaw, Johnny's life for the next two years with Jimmy Dorsey must have been less stressful, although perhaps also less stimulating.

In 1944 Guarnieri joined Raymond Scott's band at CBS. Scott also had been working with small groups drawn from his band, and many of his tone-poem compositions called for superior musicianship. The steady job gave Johnny an opportunity to work in New York jazz clubs with a variety of groups and to participate in a number of outstanding recording sessions, including a famous Savoy series with Lester Young, Billy Butterfield, Hank D'Amico, and Cozy Cole. These sides included a number of Guarnieri originals, such as "Basie English," "Exercise in Swing," and Salute to Fats." During the late 1940s and 1950s Guarnieri mainly free-lanced, with most of his time being devoted to radio and television work. In 1960 he moved to Los Angeles, where he worked at Hollywood's Plaza Hotel from 1963 to 1966.

Guarnieri died of a heart attack January 7, 1985. At that time he was still living in Hollywood where he worked nightly as a single at the Tail of the Cock restaurant. In reasonably good health until the fatal attack, he had continued to compose and record and teach a limited number of piano students. He made frequent tours to Europe and appeared at colleges and jazz festivals, and had played a concert in New Jersey the night before his death. Up until the time that this remarkable man's career ended in his sixty-seventh year, Guarnieri remained an artist of great energy who loved talking about music in all forms and welcomed any new musical challenge. Always a talented composer—he had written such pieces as "Whistle Stop," "A Gliss to Remember," "Gliss Me Again," and "Looky Here, Here's Me,"—Guarnieri continued to surprise and challenge his audiences well into his sixties, as when he began playing standards in ⅝ instead of the original ⁴⁄₄ time (for instance, in his BET album *Breakthrough*). Apparently no one ever got around to convincing Johnny Guarnieri that "old dogs can't learn new tricks."

Do you feel you're good as a musician today as you were thirty years ago?
I am a much better musician today than I was thirty years ago. Any musician who doesn't improve over that period of time ought to look for other work.

How do you account for this?
It's normal growth. A piano player is different from, let's say, a field goal kicker. A number of years ago we had a field goal kicker, George Blanda, who was still kicking for Oakland at the age of forty-three or forty-four. Everyone thought that was remarkable. Imagine someone that old still playing football. And people were amazed when Willie McCovey was still playing with the Giants at the age of forty-one. But some of our great classical musicians and composers were still going strong at twice that age, people like Pablo Casals, the cellist, who died in 1973 at the age of ninety-seven, or pianists, like Artur Rubinstein, age ninety, or Horowitz, seventy-five. Then there is Eubie Blake, who wrote "Memories of You," still playing and going strong at age ninety-six. He still appears at the Nice jazz festival about every year. In other words, music is not so much a physical thing, at least not to the extent that it is in other professions. Although I imagine if I were a trumpet player or a clarinet player, where I had to depend on my lungs or my lips, it might be more difficult to cope with being older. Doc Cheatham is well into his seventies, though, and he plays marvelously well. I recorded with him in France a few years ago. He told me when he was in Chicago back in the twenties Louis Armstrong used to send him as his substitute when he didn't feel like working a job.

What about creativity? Does it decline as people get on in years?
There is no reason why creativity should decline with age; it all depends on the individual and his particular experience. For example, I draw from many places. In my playing and writing I draw from classical music and from many popular sources. Unlike most stylists, I never was put in the position where I had to play the same way all the time. While I was doing studio work in New York City, I enjoyed the privilege of being a butterfly, going from flower to flower picking up

scents and tastes that appealed to me. I played with many fine groups
and many fine people, and I learned a lot from all of them. And I've
continued to do that. The more I play, the more I improve as a
pianist, and the more I improve as a pianist, the more I improve as a
composer and an innovator. One thing feeds another. Of course,
every jazz musician must improvise, and therefore every jazz musician
is in a sense a composer. And there is one other important thing; I
believe in God and believe that God has been awfully good to me,
giving me these great talents. I don't really pay much attention to age.
I feel like a young kid. I have everything in the world to look forward
to. I think I am going to do some very interesting things in the near
future.

*You said the other night that you had deliberately changed your style in
one respect—your move to ⁵⁄₄ time. Are there any other ways in which you are
changing your style to keep up with the times?*

No. I am not overly concerned about being contemporary. What I
have done is create as wide a repertoire of sounds and changes of pace
as possible so I can make it interesting for the listener. A lot of young
musicians come in to talk to me, and I immediately introduce them to
the great song writers, Gershwin, Kern, Cole Porter, and Fats Waller,
and as they hear this music from the past they forget about being
avant-garde and modern. All I really have to do is play the melody
and the correct sequence of chords, and they eat it up.

We have a great heritage of popular music in America, and I
don't feel that I have to do anything different or ultramodern just for
the sake of change. I may change my playing around here and there
so it doesn't get boring to the listener—or to myself. People often say,
"Johnny, you play for yourself." My usual answer is "Well, that's a good
thing, because I have very high standards." I do play for myself, and
the very best way I can. That interests me, stimulates me, and keeps
me going.

*Eddie Miller says he thinks he is playing better because he feels freer to
experiment and try new things. He feels he is not under as much pressure now,
in his older years. He says, "What does it hurt if I make a clam now and then?"*

That's right. I probably make more mistakes in one night than
most of the great drinking piano players made in their whole lives.
But then again, maybe I have attempted more dangerous things. You
can't do everything right the first time. As long as I make mistakes I
feel good, because it means I'm still striving. If a mountain climber
makes it to the top of the mountain the very first time, he's finished.

There is nothing more for him to do. That's the fun of it all—you reach one plateau, maybe fall back a little, regroup your forces, and try for a greater achievement. That's how I like to have it happen.

What do you think are the most important ingredients in good jazz performances?

First of all, there has to be sincerity, and in regard to physical assets, a good sense of time. You have to make that thing swing. That's what jazz is. When it swings, people get moved by the feeling and the emotion of the music. It's the tempo that gets them. The tempo must always be there. It may be in the background, hushed, or it may be very prominent—but jazz isn't jazz without the feeling of the beat. Although there have been some great ballad singers who have sung without pulsation, but sincerely and without tempo. And that also can be jazz.

You have to have confidence in what you do. I think that's how I managed to get the job with Benny Goodman. You have to believe in yourself. You do the best you can; that's all you can do, and if you do that, your confidence and your talents will grow. A good jazzman has to be sincere and honest, and you have to try as hard after you get a job as before you get it. Of course, that should apply whether you're a musician or an accountant or a bartender. When I go to my job at the club I play the same way every night. I'm not trying any harder to please the jazz critic than the regular customer. They are all equally important.

Are there any young people in jazz today whose work you particularly admire?

No, and I'll tell you why I say that. Even with some of those young protégés of mine, I'm afraid I have to say that they have not learned catalog. They haven't built the proper musical foundation. This is an unfortunate thing about youngsters today—they have not grown up with Cole Porter, George Gershwin, or Fats Waller. But this is something that they will have to learn on their own time. Much of their time should be spent developing a catalog. They have to give it extra effort.

When I was getting ready to record my album *Breakthrough in 5/4 Time,* I needed a bass player. I went to my good friend Don Ellis and asked him who I should use. He said he had two bass players, Jerry Napolitano and a young kid named Jim Faunt. He said he thought I ought to try Faunt. So I took him home and we rehearsed some charts. Much to my surprise, I found that he did not know the changes to "I Got Rhythm." I had to teach them to him. Now that's not his fault, but it's still a handicap.

This lack of musical depth is the reason nothing very great is coming out of most of the young people these days. Often they're great performers with great technical ability, but they will have to learn the language before they can begin to contribute anything of value. Americans always seem to want to single out someone as "the greatest." It happens all the time in sports. Every week *Down Beat* or some other trade journal will run a feature about the newest sensational piano player on the scene. We are constantly besieged with the "new greatest piano player," or "guitar player," or whatever. And the reason that they are the "greatest" is usually because they play original material. They make a big name for themselves playing numbers that nobody ever heard before, but eventually they get down to the point where they have to play "Tea for Two" or "Tiger Rag," and then they have to compete with the best in their profession. You can't go through a musical career without sooner or later putting it on the line.

What do you think of avant-garde musicians like Cecil Taylor or Ornette Coleman? Do you like the kind of thing they are doing?

I like what they are doing, although as a pianist I shouldn't judge Coleman. But I know that a lot of modern pianists do very little for me. They seem to be poetic and they often play beautifully—Bill Evans, for example. They're marvelous musicians, but they don't do much for me because they are not pulsating enough; they don't swing. I like to hear that beat. However unobtrusive it might be, I still want to hear it. I've been hearing it and enjoying it ever since I was a kid, and I'm in my sixties now. The first time I heard Fats Waller, it was his beat that got me. The same with James P. Johnson and Art Tatum. The modern pianists don't lay down the kind of beat those men did. But I can't blame the new piano players; they are living in a different world, a different time. But I enjoy listening to all the young pianists I can, and if any of them have something especially good I'll try to see if I can incorporate those ideas in what I'm doing.

How do the young musicians react to you when you play?

They seem to like it. I think they appreciate my personal dedication to my music, and I guess that shows physically. They seem to enjoy the old things even if they are not old-time jazz players themselves. And they seem to be interested in the mechanics of what I do.

Tell us a little about your daily schedule. Do you travel much? Do you work much locally?

Well, I have this wonderful job here at the Tail of the Cock. It is wonderful because I control my output of music. The hours are a bit long, 7 P.M. to 11:30 six nights a week, but then these are my practicing hours. I don't play very late compared to the early days. In New York we would start the job sometimes at seven and play until 4 A.M., and that was often seven nights a week. The money wasn't all that good then, either. And I appreciate that the management in this place backs me up on anything that takes place. We usually don't let people sing here, although I am permitted to lift that restriction from time to time. Helen Forrest comes in here now and then, and I let her sing. But for the most part we try not to have this place become a piano bar. Every year I go to Detroit, where I give concerts, and I often work a club in Toronto called George's Bourbon Street. This year I am going down to Disney World in Florida for an engagement which should be a lot of fun. And I do college dates here and there. I'm not all that busy. I'd like to be busier, but it's like getting married. You have to be asked.

To what do you attribute your longevity?

God, love, and happiness. I am happy to be alive. And if you were to ask me why I don't ever play the blues, the answer would probably be that I don't need to. My wife never ran out on me, and there have been no other big sorrows in my life. I know how to play the blues, but I don't have a need to express that kind of thing because I have a happy marriage, a loving God, and a long life filled with personal happiness.

Do you think jazz keeps you young?

I don't know if it is jazz, but I think jazz, or anything else, can keep you young if you are interested in what you are doing and if you are constantly trying to improve. You should always be looking forward to experimenting and learning. Learning is the greatest thing in the world.

What are the best and worst things about being in your sixties?

The best thing is that I am approaching an age when I have wisdom enough to put together intelligently all the lessons I have learned throughout my life so that they can do me and my friends and my customers the maximum good. My only regret is that I didn't start getting it all together sooner. I don't regret aging physically. I only regret that I didn't have the patience, tolerance, understanding, and desire many years ago that I think I have now. I guess I have always had the desire, but now it's more controlled—it's a more intelligent desire.

*Do you play because you have to financially, or mainly because you enjoy
it?*

I have to play for financial reasons. I just sold a house and could
get along very nicely for four or five years, but I don't want to do that.
I want to keep on working as long as I can.

*Is it your impression that most jazz musicians have been able to put away
nest eggs for the future?*

I have known very few musicians who were great businessmen.
And for most people in the business of playing jazz, the money has not
been all that great. When a person like me can write between five and
six thousand pieces of music and doesn't have a whopping income,
something is wrong. I've written a ton of music. Nobody knows that
better right now than my wife and the people who are helping me
move from a house to an apartment. We have already discarded
literally a ton of music paper with notes printed on it. These are
things I don't expect to use for the rest of my life, and there is simply
no room for them. I've just collected and written and collected and
written. I love to write music down. The only problem is that I have
never collected financially.

Do you think a jazz musician should ever retire?

No sir. If you do, you are not really a jazz musician. As long as I
have any ability I will not retire—at least not in the sense that Artie
Shaw retired, just gave up playing the horn. If a man becomes physically ill and can't play his instrument, that's different. But I can't
conceive of a real musician not playing any more. When you told me
last night that Jess Stacy at seventy-five is still practicing a couple of
hours a day, I felt good about it. That's the way it should be. Even if
you can't go out and perform, you still should do your thing.

Marshal Royal. Courtesy of Concord Jazz Records.

Chapter 9
Marshal Royal

If environmental influences mean anything, Marshal Royal had to become a jazz musician. For the first few years after his birth in 1912 in Sapulpa, Oklahoma, Marshal spent many nights sleeping on his father's coat behind the piano. His mother, father, and uncle had a musical group called The Three Royals, and when they played dances or private parties Marshal had to go along. He attributes his perfect pitch to all those nights behind the piano.

When Royal was four his family moved to Los Angeles, where he was launched on his musical career with a half-sized violin and a teacher who stressed a solid classical foundation. His formal instruction was supplemented at home by his father and his uncle, both of whom were music teachers as well as performers. Royal made his professional debut with the family orchestra at the age of twelve but he also had other and more profitable sources of income. In the 1920s nearly all of the theaters in the Los Angeles area held amateur nights, with first prizes usually of $25. Marshal Royal entered several of these every week, which supplemented his earnings considerably.

Upon graduating from junior high school, Royal was given a clarinet by his uncle and told that during the three-month summer vacation he would learn to play the instrument well enough to hold first chair in the high school band. His uncle gave him a lesson every day, and all that summer he practiced several hours a day. On the first day of school, Marshal auditioned on clarinet and won first chair in the high school band. He also was first chair (concert master) in the violin section of the high school orchestra, which may account for the title of a recent solo album (with rhythm section) for Concord Records, *First Chair*.

After mastering the clarinet, Royal took up alto saxophone, and during his high school years worked regularly at one of Los Angeles's biggest nightclubs, the Apex, with Curtis Mosby's Blue Blowers. A fellow sideman on that band was Lawrence Brown, who later became famous as a star trombone soloist with Duke Ellington. In the early 1930s Royal and Brown joined the Les Hite band, working at Frank Sebastian's New Cotton Club in Los Angeles. This band, which had Lionel Hampton on drums and vibes, was often fronted by Fats Waller or Louis Armstrong. Some of Marshal Royal's earliest recordings were with this band, including the Armstrong hit "Confessin'" in 1930. Royal stayed with Hite during most of the 1930s, although he also played with the Duke Ellington band in 1930, 1933, and 1934, when they came west to do Hollywood films.

In 1940 Marshal Royal joined the newly formed Lionel Hampton band, where he was also featured on clarinet in the Hampton sextet. In 1942 Royal went into the navy. After his discharge he spent several years doing studio work in Hollywood and playing with a variety of small groups, such as those of Eddie Heywood, Slim Gaillard, and Jack McVea. In 1951 Royal replaced Buddy De Franco on clarinet in the Count Basie septet, and the next year helped Basie reform his big band. Royal remained with the Basie organization for nearly twenty years as lead alto man and musical director. He not only was one of the finest section men in the business, but also an excellent soloist, both sweet and hot. Royal was virtually the leader of the band during those twenty years, serving as a father figure for most of the sidemen.

After leaving the Basie band in 1970, Royal decided to settle down. He worked as lead alto man in the Coconut Grove house band, and played a variety of television shows. He still enjoys working jazz festivals with his old boss Lionel Hampton, and he occasionally tours Europe with jazz groups comprising old friends from his Basie days. But he prefers spending as much time as possible at home with his lovely wife, a former professional singer. Royal has little trouble finding work close to home. He plays lead alto with the Capp-Pierce Juggernaut and the Bill Berry L.A. Big Band. Royal's reputation as a section leader is such that his solo efforts often have gone unnoticed. In 1960 he did cut a record as featured soloist with Gordon Jenkins, but because of poor distribution his special talents did not become widely appreciated by the jazz public. However, in 1978 and 1980 Concord issued two albums, the aforementioned *First Chair,* and *Royal Blue,* both of which featured Royal's solo horn with a four-man rhythm section. His performance on these albums on a group of old standards and Marshal Royal originals testifies to his undiminished artistry.

When did you start learning to play music?

I have been learning music all my life. My father was a musician, my mother was a musician, and my uncle was a musician. I had an instrument—a half-size violin—as soon as I was big enough to hold it. I started studying when I was four years old. I was fortunate—music was easy for me. I lived music every day. From the time I could talk, my folks had me humming melodies. Music has been a part of my life for a very long time.

You are now sixty-seven years old. Are you as good a jazz musician today as you were at thirty-seven?

I think so. A lot depends on your outlook and whether or not you have an open mind. If I were a person with a closed mind, I would have been satisfied with the way I played thirty-five or forty years ago, and I would ignore everything that is happening today. But I have always tried to progress. I think that was one of the important things my parents taught me—to be constantly studying and learning new ways of doing things. Perhaps I am not quite as outgoing as when I was younger, but overall I think that the knowledge and experience I have acquired over the years have been a tremendous advantage. If you make use of that experience and keep in command of your instrument and know what you want to do, there is no reason your ability should decline after the age of fifty or sixty or whatever someone decides is the line of demarcation between young and old. As long as you stay around younger people and try to think young, age is only a number. Creativity shouldn't be any more of a problem for someone over sixty-five than for someone younger.

What is the role of experience?

You have more ideas to draw upon. Lack of experience is a great handicap for most of the young people who are coming into the music business today. They have no repertoire, no background. They don't know how to play for dances because they don't know what a dance is. They don't know how to play shows because they have had no experience playing shows. The average person who comes into the business today has had the benefit of three or four years of college study, and while a lot of them can play the hell out of their horns, they can't play music. They don't know what music is. Many of the rehearsal bands around town try to get me to come to their rehearsals to work with their sax sections, because most of the guys don't know anything about playing lead and playing the melody. Very few of them have had a concert education, and you learn how to play melodies by playing concerts. You have to learn how to get feeling, how to handle your highs and lows. You have to learn how to meld tones, how to sweeten them, how to change vibratos, and how to use two or three types of vibrato. You also have to learn how to emulate the human voice. Some of these things come with legitimate study, but many of them have to be learned through experience. There are many good college programs, but many of the teachers' backgrounds are only teaching. Many a good college saxophone teacher has not had enough experience playing lead alto or solo alto with a band to be able to help a student who wants to play with a jazz orchestra.

Do you see age as representing any kind of handicap at all to jazz performance?

Only in regard to energy level. When you get older you don't always have the push you need. But then, as you grow older you have to learn how to conserve energy so you won't waste it. A lot of kids put out twice as much energy as it really takes to do the job. Putting out effort doesn't necessarily mean that the quality will be improved. You have to know how to take advantage of your resources. As you grow older you try to make everything count; you don't give anything away. In music it's like in chemistry. Once you get a solution saturated, it's saturated. If you put in more you only oversaturate it, you don't improve the quality. When you start getting older you begin to learn where to cut it off. And sometimes you end up doing a whole lot more using a lot less energy.

Do you still practice daily?

No, I don't practice. I practiced when I was a child—sometimes six, eight, ten hours a day, because I loved to play. My parents didn't really have to force me to practice, because I wanted to play.

Musicians sometimes get depressed at the way they sound, and they start experimenting with new mouthpieces or new reeds. Do you experience any of these problems?

I worked that out many years ago. I decided that I was going to play the horn, and the horn was not going to play me. Some fellows that have been playing for years will change mouthpieces two or three times during the course of a year. I've been playing one mouthpiece now for over twenty years, and I am not going to change. If that one should break or warp, I would try to get one as much like it as possible. I also have the same horn now, a Conn, that I bought brand-new in 1932. I have had other horns offered to me free over the years, but my old silver Conn is the only horn I care for. It's a particular model. Conn sent me a new model a few years back, but I gave it back. I just had my 1932 horn overhauled last week. I had it all refurbished, and it's ready to go.

Are you playing any differently now from the way you did thirty years ago?

I don't believe that I am doing anything radically different from what I always did. The scales and harmonic ideas are pretty much the same as they used two hundred years ago. What's different today is that we're extending those scales and creating new modes of music. When I first started in this business, the arrangements we bought [stocks] only had three saxophone parts, and people became accustomed to hearing the 1-3-5. Then around the mid-1930s they started to add an additional saxophone. With that addition, people began to hear the sixth of the chord. The horns were playing the 1-3-5-6. People just grew accustomed to these sound changes; a lot of them didn't even know it was happening. Later we got five- and six-part harmonies. Then people had to adjust to the new sounds of these harmonies. You couldn't use tone clusters in the old days, because people's ears were not educated to hear and enjoy them. They would have thought that there was dissonance, that someone was playing the wrong note.

A lot of younger musicians are playing different types of scales, different kinds of arpeggios and different kinds of rhythms (like double-time tempos), but it often takes a trained musician to decide whether or not they are doing anything worthwhile. A lot of people today are playing things clear out of the skies just to be different, just to make an impression. I don't like to judge, however. People used to put Stravinsky down, but in the end he showed them that he knew what he was doing.

Is your playing affected by what the young people are doing?
No. I don't believe I am affected at all by younger players.

Are there any young saxophone players that you admire?
I like all good sax players that can really play. I like them all, because I think that every guy who is a good player has something to offer. But I don't know of any perfect players anywhere. I've never heard a perfect player in my life, and I'm not one who goes out and looks for people to idolize. I've never done that. For example, I never was a record collector, because I always figured if I was to listen to another man's record too long I would end up imitating him to some

extent. I guess I was just vain enough to figure I had enough to offer myself so that I didn't have to copy someone else.

What do you think of Ornette Coleman?
I haven't been able to adjust to him at all. As far as his saxophone playing goes, I have always thought that he was striving for something or trying to capture something, but that what he was trying to capture was very, very elusive. And I don't think he has ever found what he was looking for.

What do you think are the major components in expert jazz performance?
I think the main thing in jazz performance is preparation. The guy who is going to play jazz should have a perfect knowledge of his instrument, and also of all the chords and the chord change progressions. He should know inversions. I believe the jazz musician should have some classical background, and of course he should have some idea of what he is going to play. Although, of course, jazz is extemporaneous playing; I don't ever play a solo twice in the same way. If I tried to work out everything about a solo in advance, it would come out too tight.

Another important thing is you want to communicate to the listener what you are trying to do. And while you have to plan ahead, you also have to make sure the result doesn't sound staged or rehearsed. When I did my recent album *First Chair,* we worked with tunes I had never recorded before, but had been playing most of my life. I told the fellows what I wanted to play and what key, and we just played, with no music.

Some people believe that musicians and artists in general can no longer be creative after the age of sixty-five or seventy. How would you respond to that?
The only person who would say that is one who has never been sixty-five. It is a very curious attitude, however. As long as you continue to open your eyes every morning, you have to work out creative ways of dealing with life. Just living can involve creativity. Every day that the sun comes up life will be a little bit different than it was the day before and will require new adjustments. How can anybody who is not yet sixty-five know what it is like to be past that age? Creativity can involve how you think and relate to the world around you, and no one knows the problems until they've got there themselves.

Some of the older musicians are getting more attention than ever these days. Dexter Gordon came back from Europe and is enjoying great popularity.
It makes me laugh to hear you refer to Dexter Gordon as one of

the older musicians. I gave him his first job. I guess that makes me ancient.

I'm talking about jazz musicians who were popular during the thirties and forties and then lost out when rock came in. Do you anticipate a revival for these people?

Of course, they never really disappeared. Most of them have been working consistently, fifty-two weeks a year, every year, somewhere. From the time that I started we've had three or four generations of audiences. Every ten or twelve years there is a new group of people who are discovering jazz. What to us is old is brand-new to these kids. You hear that the big bands may be coming back; of course, they never went away. They're not around in the numbers there were during the thirties, but a few have survived. There just weren't too many people listening to them. Some have maintained a public over the years—Count Basie, Duke Ellington, Stan Kenton, Lionel Hampton, Woody Herman. A lot of kids in their teens are now hearing sounds from the past, but these sounds are brand-new to them. I think that right now there are more kids who have heard of me than there were twenty years ago—especially in Europe. In both Europe and Japan kids twelve to fourteen years old are knowledgeable about jazz and jazz artists. They know what to appreciate—when to applaud and when to keep quiet. They know what's happening.

What would you like to see happen to jazz in America in the next ten years?

I don't think anything needs to happen to jazz in the next ten years except to find somebody to listen to it. I'd just like to see the audience get bigger.

What kinds of jobs do you play? Are they mostly in Los Angeles, or do you also travel?

I seldom travel anymore; I mostly do recording jobs and TV work. I play big band concerts, and now and then I play private parties, but I am selective about those. I guess I pretty much run the whole gamut, but I don't do one-nighters anymore. In a year I'll probably play five or six jazz concerts. I'd like to do more of these. They don't take much of your time, they pay very well, and they are class jobs. They also help sell your records. I often do the North Sea Festival, the Montrose Festival, and the festival in Nice. Then I hit the Concord Jazz Festival, and I also do the Dick Gibson Festival at the Broadmoor in Colorado Springs over Labor Day. I have been asked several times to get into the clinic deal, go around from school to school teaching about playing saxophone in a big jazz ensemble. I think I could really help some of the kids if I started it, but I don't know if I want to put my nose to the grindstone that much.

Some people my age get into so many things they're running from one thing to another almost like the old one-nighters. I don't want that. I'd rather get two or three studio calls a week and know who I'm going to be playing with. It also isn't good to get tied up in some of these long-running TV shows. I don't want to get tied down to anything that I don't really like to do. I like to play when things will be enjoyable. When things are enjoyable it takes absolutely no effort at all to do it.

As you grow older, have you developed any physical problems—such as hearing loss—that affect your ability to play?

No, I have all my faculties. I hear good and I only use glasses to read fine print. I usually don't wear glasses to play, either, unless I'm unfamiliar with the music, or the lighting is bad. I think that once you start using glasses your vision automatically changes, and you become dependent on them.

What are the best and the worst things about getting older?

The best thing is that by my age you should know most of the answers. The worst thing is getting up the energy to use your acquired knowledge effectively.

You appear to be in excellent physical shape. To what do you attribute your longevity?

I have always done everything in moderation and I have never used narcotics. I drank, and I still drink, but I can take it or leave it. I used to be a slave to cigarettes—smoked three packs a day for years. One day about ten years ago I decided I had had enough nicotine, so I just threw the cigarettes out the window and I have never smoked another. Once I quit, everybody said now you are going to get fat. But I fooled them there too. I immediately lost fifteen pounds.

Do you jog or do anything like that?

No. I had a bone spur on my spine in 1974 and it temporarily numbed both my legs to a certain extent. But now it's almost normal again. I have done that by walking the golf course and carrying my own bag. I hunt and fish too. I have always done these things, and I have always tried to keep myself in good physical condition. When I was a kid I lifted weights and I played all the sports. I can still play many of them pretty good—except those that involve fast sprints. I can't get up to fast sprints anymore.

Are you a day person or a night person?
I was a night person all my life, but now I have suddenly become a day person. I wake up practically at daybreak and get up and begin reading the paper by six-thirty or seven. I work very few late jobs now. As a matter of fact, there aren't many of those kinds of jobs around anymore. The liquor law here insists on a 2 A.M. closing in nightclubs. But then I don't play many nightclubs anymore either. I just don't go for all that stompin' and jumpin' and rompin' anymore. Most of my playing takes place in the daytime now. I like daytime. I like to enjoy every hour of the daylight that I possibly can.

Do you think that a jazz musician should ever retire?
I don't think musicians should really retire at all. Being a musician is a little different from other kinds of jobs. There aren't many jobs in this world where you can perform three or four hours a night and make a living at it. You're not like a working man that does manual labor, or an accountant that has to sit for eight hours a day working on the company's books. Being a jazz musician puts you somewhat in the artist category. You have a lot of freedom to do what you want to. Take me, for example—I am not retired. I am just winding down gradually. I try to keep active, because I know if I quit I'll go batty. The question for me is, retire to what? There isn't anything I like to do more than play music.

A lot of jazz musicians keep working after sixty-five because of money problems. Would you be financially able to quit?
My wife and I are fairly comfortable, and she is mainly responsible for that. She kept a home going for me while I was on the road with Count Basie. I made sure that the house payments were always made and that she was well taken care of. It was important that I have a place to go to when I left the road, so we turned over a couple of pieces of property, and we put some into savings. I invested in the stock market a bit too, and did a little investing here and there—mostly the kind of sensible investments that middle-aged people tend to go into.

The music business is a lot different today than it used to be. When a musician got to be thirty-five or forty years old, he used to be considered an old dude and technically washed up. People that age usually went into some other profession. In 1959 the musicians union came up for the first time with a retirement plan. It was a forced-payment arrangement, but it still isn't followed by all locals in the United States. If a decent sort of plan had been established many years ago, all the guys that worked twenty or thirty years would have themselves a retirement of several hundred dollars a year for the rest of their lives. The young musicians today will have such a fund after they retire thirty years from now.

A number of the older jazz musicians we have interviewed express deep religious convictions. Are you religious?

I'm not one of those out-and-out religious freaks. I was raised a Christian Scientist; that was the church I attended as a child. To be a Christian Scientist requires quite a bit of study. It teaches you how to have power over your mind. I find it a very clean and lovely religion in many ways; you learn to think and to know yourself. When I was out on the road doing one-nighters I got away from the church, but I still know my roots and I respect them. I respect all religions. Any religion that can help a person is worthwhile; I will jump with both feet into the corner of that religion. I try not to put down any religion, but I'm not one of those people who has to jump up every Sunday and run off to church. I learned how to pray within myself as a child, and that is the life that I try to lead now.

Howard Rumsey. Courtesy of *Easy Reader*, Hermosa Beach. Photo by Cary Simon.

Chapter 10
Howard Rumsey

Howard Rumsey was born on November 7, 1917 in Brawley, California, a small town in the desert of the Imperial Valley. Neither of his parents were musicians, but his father liked music, bought Howard a piano, and found him a piano teacher. His mother made him practice. During his high school years he learned to play the drums, and he became a member of the municipal band and also played in a saloon after the repeal of Prohibition (which occurred in his senior year). When Howard went to Los Angeles City College, he hoped to finance his schooling by playing dance jobs around Los Angeles. Advised to take up bass because there was a shortage of bass players, he did just that.

During his second year at City College in 1938, Rumsey met Jack Ordean, an alto sax player and a friend of Vido Musso, who had just left the Benny Goodman band. Musso was forming a band and Howard was asked to join as its bassist; the piano player would be Stan Kenton. The Vido Musso band was very short-lived and was ultimately taken over by Gus Arheim, who moved it to San Francisco. Howard Rumsey and Stan Kenton returned to Los Angeles, where they auditioned for the band of a rising movie personality, Johnny "Scat" Davis, the *Hurray for Hollywood* man. Both were invited to join the band, but only Rumsey accepted the offer. He spent the next year and a half touring the United States in Johnny Scat's double-decker bus. Upon returning to Los Angeles in 1941, Rumsey was asked to join the new Stan Kenton band, which was working at the Rendezvous Ballroom in Balboa. Rumsey played electric bass in that band (perhaps in self-defense, since the group had been labeled the "loudest in captivity"). His use of amplification was undoubtedly unique in 1941.

Described by George T. Simon as "a tremendous bassist," Howard

97

Rumsey was well known for his "Concerto for Doghouse," an early solo bass performance that became almost as famous as Bobby Haggart's "Big Noise from Winnetka." In her book *Straight Ahead* (1973) Carol Easton remembered the twenty-three-year-old Kenton bass player as "a skinny, naive country kid . . . who attacked his then-unorthodox electric bass with such convulsive ferocity that he was dubbed The Flying Spider" (1973:59).

Rumsey's tenure with Kenton ended in 1942, but his reputation as an outstanding bass man brought him a series of jobs with such well-known organizations as those of Freddie Slack, Barney Bigard, Alvino Rey, Charlie Barnet, Wingy Manone, and Johnny Richards. In 1949 Rumsey embarked on a remarkable experiment, as he explained to Leonard Feather:

> I had originally seen the Lighthouse when it was a restaurant called Verpilates'. I had always liked the idea of a place where you could jam until all hours and people would just sit around and listen. I came back to Hermosa Beach and found that there was nothing of that kind there, but Verpilates' now had a new name and band-stand—but no music. I walked in there one Saturday afternoon and saw John Levine, the owner, and about nineteen people sitting around the bar. I asked him, "Did you ever think about having a session here on Sunday?" He wound up agreeing to try it out. The Sunday sessions were an immediate hit. It was a case of being in the right place at the right time. (1966a:6)

Howard Rumsey's groups (known as the Lighthouse All-Stars) parlayed the Sunday sessions into performances six nights a week and featured such jazz stars as Chet Baker, Gerry Mulligan, Shelley Manne, Sonny Criss, Shorty Rogers, Jimmy Giuffre, Bob Cooper (a regular), Bud Shank, Hampton Hawes, Frank Rosolino, and Bob Brookmeyer. Not only did Rumsey's groups keep jazz alive during a period of rock and roll domination, they also evolved an original jazz style, altogether known as West Coast Jazz.

While at first the town of Hermosa Beach took a dim view of the Lighthouse and its beboppers, in time Rumsey became known as one of its foremost citizens, with friends at City Hall, the Chamber of Commerce, and the Lion's Club. In a *Down Beat* interview with John Tynan in 1958, Rumsey discussed his civic responsibilities. He said, "Before an artist can assume his proper social position he must be considered on a level with the other leading citizens in his community. He quite literally has got to take his place among the community leaders" (1958:15).

Rumsey is an unusual combination of artist and entrepreneur. In 1966 Leonard Feather wrote in *International Musician*, "Both as a musician and as a business man he keeps up with current events and looks forward eagerly to whatever the future may bring. It is unfortunate for our business that there are not more musicians with the initiative, courage, and persistence of Hermosa Beach's most celebrated adopted son, Howard Rumsey." (1966:29)

Today Howard Rumsey is the proprietor of a Redondo Beach club known as Concerts by the Sea. The club is designed as a concert hall, with a stage up front and seats in rows, as in an auditorium. A narrow shelf on the back of each seat holds customers' drinks and food, but waitresses are not permitted to serve during sets. The club is a performers' paradise, with little or no room noise, good acoustics and an excellent sound system, a well-tuned grand piano, and a boss who enjoys every performance as much as the customers and performers do. Rumsey's choice of talent to play his club is an important aspect of its success. He has the knack of sensing which new young talent to support without succumbing to the commercialism that has plagued the jazz world during the last decade. He books traditional jazz groups too. All the performers he presents, of whatever style, are received enthusiastically by a loyal group of regulars. He dreams of opening a chain of jazz clubs across the country, so that everyone can participate in the excitement and pleasure of jazz, our national music.

Do you still play your bass, now that you're in your sixties?

No, not lately. I started out as a kid playing piano for eight years, and I played drums and trumpet, and then I went to the string bass for thirty years. Now I have two basses left. I have my practice bass here at the office and I have a good bass at home, but mainly I just look at them. Every once in a while I'll play some little thing. What I am doing now is practicing ukelele so that I can play when I'm by myself.

Then you have no future performance plans?

No. There isn't anybody that can hire me—I'm the most expensive bass player in town. My salary is prohibitive. But seriously, I have a better job now—providing the proper context for good musicians to be heard—in a setting where they can get their message across. And that's a big job at this time. But as far as my being a musician is concerned, I was just floored when the union sent me a thirty-year card recently, because I never really decided to be a musician. It just happened. I figured that if you can't decide in thirty years that you are going to be a musician, it is time to quit. The last time I performed was with Dizzy Gillespie. His bass player didn't show up on time, so he asked me to step in. I had a bad time and figured that was a real fine way to retire.

Some of the traditional jazz people are in more demand now than ever before. What do you think accounts for this?

Sacramento has the largest traditional jazz festival in the world. Literally hundreds of Dixieland and swing players come there from all over the world. I don't quite understand the popularity of some of these people, in the light of the commercial bombardment of the current styles, but there is almost an underground movement to keep them alive. And I definitely think these old-time players have a special function today. It is awfully important to know where the music came from. When I started this club, my second attraction was The World's Greatest Jazz Band, and then I went even further back, to Earl Hines. I wanted to start with the soul and roots of jazz, and then come forward from there.

You know, many of the earlier players were white, whereas most of the stars today are black, and it just isn't right for blacks to claim that jazz is their music. There is no question but that the majority of jazz greats have been black, but I hate to see history distorted by neglecting all those early white jazz musicians. I am concerned because I have always loved playing the music so much. You need history, because you can never go forward unless you know where you came from. That is why it is so important to have the older guys still around, still playing their music.

Do you think jazz has a chance of staging a comeback in America?

Oh, definitely. *Fortune* magazine recently carried a story on executives who get together and play in a big jazz ensemble as a pastime. Over in Century City there is a gentleman who sponsors a jam session one day a week, and the executives come out of their offices with their horns and play. The same thing is going on in New York. And the schools are helping jazz along too. Almost 90 percent of the young people these days are student musicians of one kind or another—there are some fine high school jazz ensembles. Stan Kenton camps and other summer workshops for young musicians all over the United States are turning out musicians of professional caliber. Maybe they aren't all going to become professional musicians—the percentage will probably be very, very low—but they are going to have an appreciation of good music their whole lives, and they are always going to feel that they are part musician.

How do the young musicians who come into your club respond to you as an old-timer from the swing tradition?

They seem to like it. But I don't come on strong with these guys. Most of them know me through my association with the Lighthouse;

that goes back some twenty years. I put a lot of these guys in business. Take Roy Harris, whose band was here just recently. He was working in a parking lot in downtown Los Angeles. He would finish work at night, drive out to the Lighthouse, take out his vibes, put them on the bandstand, and be ready to play in six minutes. And he would be playing the rest of the night. Guys don't forget our earlier associations. Les McCann and Max Roach are good friends too. I got Max out here in 1962.

How do you evaluate some of our more far-out or experimental musicians today?

I think that every musician that makes a name for himself today—somebody like Ornette Coleman, Cecil Taylor, or Anthony Braxton—first has to become controversial so that he gets talked about. Take Miles Davis, for example. He is the only guy I know that parlayed what he couldn't do into a fortune. He never could play the trumpet like Diz or any straight-out trumpet player. He had that eggshell-thin tone and those long pauses. He couldn't even talk, and he parlayed that too. He became the silent one. But he started a whole new trend.

When Anthony Braxton came out here to play a job in my club some time ago he and Major Holling were rehearsing one night and they started to play "All the Things You Are." It really sounded good. I mean they were playing that tune like it should be played, no ifs, ands, or buts. It was down. It was there. But they never played "All the Things You Are" again during their whole engagement. It wasn't that they couldn't play inside, it was that they didn't want to. They just did it to let me know they could play the tune, but it wasn't their thing. Their gig wasn't a commercial success, but it was a very interesting engagement. Guys were catering to their inner desires to create whatever came off the top of their head, and they did some very creative things. People talk about freedom—that is the real essence of it.

What is required for good jazz performance?

Let me answer that first as a club owner trying to provide the best environment possible for the artists, and secondly as a musician who has worked with a lot of very talented jazz performers and who has heard some great improvisation. First, you need a really good keyboard—a Steinway or some other concert keyboard. Then you need a room with great acoustics, where the sound doesn't bounce around. You have to make sure that the audience can hear the music but aren't slugged by it, so they can take in the music and then reflect their feelings back to the band. Next, you need musicians that are really talented and can actually create, can make a spontaneous statement. They can't be just reciting a memorized thing, or there will be nothing alive about it, and they won't be able to transmit anything worthwhile to the audience. After all this is put together, then three more things have to happen. The musicians have to be paid adequately—not too much, not too little; the audience needs to leave the performance feeling they got their money's worth, and the club operator needs to make a reasonable profit.

Now, from the standpoint of a musician, I pride myself on being able to appreciate really good jazz playing. That's why I'm in business, because I've been able to recognize good from bad and can give the public the best that's around today.

Let me tell you about quality. Bob Brookmeyer has a new record that was recorded live in a club in Boston, Sandy's. The instrumentation is drums, guitar, bass, and trombone. They were just playing standards, and mostly they were playing the melody just like the composer wrote it. Then all of a sudden Brookmeyer changes three or four notes. He changes the melodic line just enough to make it actually better than the composer wrote it, and you think to yourself, "Why the hell didn't the composer think of that?" As I listened to these four guys, I thought that someone should give them doctorate degrees. The more I listened, the more I realized that their time was different too. It wasn't stretching out or bogging down; it was all sitting up all the time. It even sounded like they were turning the time around. The music sounded fresh and vibrant. Then I thought, these people don't need doctorate degrees; they are already the teachers, the masters. And so much depends on how much they know about the music. If you don't have a classical background or training, you can't do these kinds of creative, imaginative things.

Most of the jazz musicians today are first-generation players; I'm one. There never was a musician in my family. The only hope for a first-generation player is education, and that means he is going to have to study theory and technique and listen to good music. There is no other way. You take a guy like Fiedler—fifty years conductor of the Boston Pops. There is a musician. I admire anyone who is that well educated. But where you go from there is up to you.

What would you like to see happen to jazz in the next ten years?

I'd like to see fifty rooms like this one at Concerts By the Sea; I'd like to put together a chain of restaurants and rotate the musical talent from place to place. Each restaurant would have two floors and an open area in the middle for the band. On the upper level you could have a family-type restaurant where people could bring their children and have an inexpensive meal, see the musicians through glass and hear them through controllable volume speakers. It could be a volume-type operation, with no saloon atmosphere. On the ground floor you could have your saloon and your concert atmosphere. Neither group of clients would bother the other. The thing that all good players abhor most is room noise. If you could fix it so there is no room noise, then you would really get a great concert.

What is your daily routine?

The first thing I do in the morning is try to get in tune mentally with a little religious reading. I am a Christian Scientist; I have been since I was seven years old. It's a delightful, workable religion for me. I have never told anyone that they should be a Christian Scientist, and I've never told anyone that they should listen to jazz. I just hire people and put their names out front, and the people who want to hear them come in and have a good time.

After my morning religious reading, I have various things to do for relaxation. I live in Torrance and have a sailboat in a harbor about fifteen minutes away. I also have an airplane at the Torrance airport, about five minutes away. Besides flying and sailing, I play some golf. And my home is really a paradise for me; it's surrounded by trees a hundred years old, and there are possums and skunks and lots of birds around the place. Since I have to be here at the club every night, I spend as much time as possible enjoying myself during the day. This place is a consistent money-maker, which enables me to relax and enjoy my sailing, golfing, and flying during the day and my listening to good jazz at night. The reason you don't find more guys like me in business is because they are too interested in the next buck. I guess I can't blame them for that—it seems like nobody can ever find enough money to do what they want to do. But if I can pay my bills, keep the landlord happy, keep the city happy, and keep the law enforcement agencies happy, then I think I am doing O.K.

Do you have a regular exercise program to help you stay healthy?

No, but I do walk a lot, and I play golf and tennis and I sail. You can get quite a workout sailing. I don't smoke. I quit that a long time ago, and I drink very little—a glass of brandy once in a while and wine with dinner occasionally. I have never worried much about calories, although I am starting to now. I've gained about twelve pounds in the last couple of years; I'm up to 204, and I have to watch it. I like to eat. My parents were in the restaurant business, and I love restaurants. I know every good one for miles around. But my wife Joyce rides herd on me. We have been married for twenty-seven years. She isn't a musician, but she really enjoys good music. She knows the lyrics and melodies to almost all of the standard tunes of the thirties and forties. It just thrills me. I wish I could do that. She works here with me, handling the money, which relieves me of that responsibility.

Do you ever plan to retire?

Well, there's fourteen years left on my lease at the club here, but I don't think in those terms. I don't do much planning; all my life I've just let things happen—like my music career, for example. I've been very fortunate most of my life—family responsibilities have never forced me to go in a given direction. My father gave me a musical education, and then he passed away when I was seventeen. He never heard me play or realized what he had done for me, and my mother was never interested in music.

Music is a bit different from most jobs; people seem less likely to credit you with a job well done when it's retirement time. I used to work with Jack Jenny during the war. He was a genius, and I think that man died of a broken heart. I used to take him home after work at night, and he'd have me drop him off a block from his house. He was living with his in-laws, and he didn't want to disturb them. They couldn't stand musicians. Isn't that something? But I guess that's par for the course. Just like the tragedy with Bix, the whole scene keeps repeating itself over and over.

You seem relatively comfortable financially. Do you think you are typical of jazz musicians your age?

That's a hard question. I really don't know anybody who isn't in good shape compared to what it was like when I first was in the business. Personally, I've been pretty lucky all along. I had some tough times for a while at first. I had no money and nothing to eat, but then I managed to go to work, and I have never been out of work since. I've never drawn an unemployment check.

I don't think it's that way with all the older musicians, however. Take somebody like Johnny Guarnieri, who plays out at the Tail of the Cock. He works the cocktail and dinner hour. I don't know whether people appreciate what a great musician he is when they find him in that setting. And Johnny isn't just a great musician, he is a musicologist if I ever saw one. He ought to be subsidized by the government so he would never have to worry about bill one. He is a straight-out genius.

I think it is a crime the way America treats its great artists. When I was in high school and started playing in my town in the Imperial Valley, the joint I worked in sometimes brought in old pros to work the gigs. One guy didn't even have a place to sleep one night, so I took him home and he stayed at my house. When I came to L.A. to go to college, I got into the Kenton clique accidentally through this guy Jack Ordean, their lead alto player, who was brilliant. [George Simon wrote about Ordean in *Metronome* (1971:175): "It's a thrilling alto, too; one of the surest and yet most exciting . . . to hit jazz in many a moon. This Ordean is one man whose conceptions you're going to hear plenty of from now on."] Jack just died recently. Everything in the world happened to him in his later years. He was on disability; he was sick and had nothing. Finally he had to go to a Veterans Hospital. When Matty Matlock, the great Crosby band clarinetist, passed away, they had to have a big benefit to pay for his funeral and pay up his debts. And when Blue Mitchell died they had a big blowout at the musicians union, where they collected $8,000 for his widow. That's the state of affairs in Lower Slobbovia.

In America the music business grows like a bush in a vacant lot. It grows when there is water on it, but nobody takes care of it. Some years it almost withers away and dies, and then it perks up again when it gets a bit more attention. There is really no rhyme or reason to it. In the jazz music business there always seems to be a crisis. A while back I had Milt Jackson's group in here for a week, and we were off 40 percent in our profits. The following week I had L.A. Ford, and we were off 50 percent. At that point I was thinking to myself, "This is it." But then I think this at least once every year. I've decided now that it is going to keep rolling forever, no matter what. The thing to do is to have inner confidence, and don't push it. Let it happen. And it will.

Although you are no longer playing, you seem to be very much a part of the jazz world. Do you enjoy this side of the business?

Yes, I'm glad to be on this side of it now. Because I was never a money player, I was just a fun player, and there is no room for a fun player these days. But when I hear somebody good play, it really knocks me out. That makes it all worthwhile. That's why I get a kick out of helping guys who really need it. It's tough to make it these days. It terrifies me to think of all the people who put their heart and soul into the music and studied and practiced and played, and then came out on the losing side in the end. To see what has happened to some of these excellent musicians just terrifies me. I guess that's one of the reasons I'm running a club now, instead of trying to make it with my bass. I guess I don't have the temperament to be a money player.

Lawrence Brown. Courtesy of Stanley Dance.

Chapter 11
Lawrence Brown

Lawrence Brown was named after the Kansas university town in which he was born in August 1905 to a family in which his minister father led the congregational singing, his mother played the organ, and the kids all sang in the choir. The Browns soon moved to Pasadena, California, where Lawrence experimented with a variety of instruments—piano, violin, tuba, and finally trombone. He admits that as a teenager he was attracted by the popularity of "tailgate" trombone, but as he perfected his skill he began to be repulsed by the smeared tailgate sound, which was mainly used for comic effect. Believing that the trombone deserved better than merely supplying comic relief in a Dixieland band, Brown embarked on a prolonged period of serious study. After graduation from high school, he enrolled in Pasadena Junior College, intending to study medicine. While in college he played numerous engagements with local orchestras and eventually became a regular at the Little Cotton Club in Culver City, playing with the Les Hites Band (with Lionel Hampton on drums) and with many of the other bands booked into the club for limited engagements, including one with Louis Armstrong. Here he established his unique style, which has been called "warm," "smooth," and "very melodious."

One night in 1932 Irving Mills heard Brown play at the Cotton Club and talked Duke Ellington into adding him to the band, which was playing a short engagement at the Orpheum Theater in Los Angeles. A few days later, when the Ellington band left for the East Coast, Lawrence Brown went with them. But for weeks he wasn't permitted to play because he made the thirteenth member of the band, and the superstitious Duke made him wait until a fourteenth, Otto Hardwicke, joined the group. Brown received no salary while he was waiting. Then when he finally joined the others, he found that there were no parts written for him, so he created his own first trombone music by doubling the first trumpet part an octave lower.

Brown stayed with the Duke until 1951, when he left to play with the Johnny Hodges Band. After a four-year stint with Hodges, he worked as a studio musician for CBS in New York, where he played jobs ranging from symphony work to recording with Jackie Gleason. In the 1960s he returned to the Ellington orchestra, where he remained until his retirement in 1970.

During Brown's tenure with the Duke he attracted a great deal of attention from the critics, who described his playing as "charming and delicate" (Hugues Panassié) or "sentimental," "over-emphatic," and "legato and highly melodic in his improvisations" (Leonard Feather). In 1934 Panassié compared Brown to Jack Teagarden, Miff Mole, and Tommy Dorsey, maintaining that:

> He is a musician whose temperament is well suited to mild, delicate interpretations. He is not built for that hot playing in fast time which calls for a fiery, forceful performance. It is not that he lacks the necessary instrumental technique; on the contrary, he is one of the most astonishing trombone virtuosos. In a slow or moderate tempo, he will occasionally—in the midst of some mild, rather sentimental solo—improvise the most fantastic passages quite of the level with Jack Teagarden at his best. That "tension" in his tone and the high quality of his inspiration (his phrases are always perfectly constructed) makes Lawrence Brown one of the best hot musicians. (1934:83)

The performances usually considered his best while with the Duke were on "Ducky Wucky" (1932) and "Rose of Rio Grande" (1938). Brown often recorded with small groups drawn from the Ellington Orchestra and cut at least one record, *Inspired Abandon,* with a group under his own name. After his retirement from music in 1970, he had several osteoplastic operations, which ended his playing career. But he has served on numerous committees at the Los Angeles Musicians Union, and he rents from Nellie Lutcher, the pianist of "Hurry on Down to My House, Baby" fame.

This man is the only one of the dozen elderly musicians we interviewed who had retired almost entirely from the profession. Brown's troubled relationship with Duke Ellington seems to have left him with a bitterness that has colored his whole outlook on jazz and its artists.

As Panassié wrote in 1934:

> Duke's band requires soloists who can adapt their inspiration to that of their leader, and Lawrence Brown has too much personality—or,

if you prefer to say so, a personality too different from that of the Duke—to yield easily to these demands. He was not meant for this particular orchestra, and his playing often seems complicated and artificial because of the constraint he puts on himself or which is imposed upon him. Near Ellington, his personality cannot expand. (1934:84)

In this interview we learn what it is like financially to be a retired jazz artist, and what Brown's many years in jazz taught him about what goes into the making of a creative artist.

How long has it been since you retired?

I haven't touched a horn since 1970. At that time I just quit. I'm a little reluctant to talk about what prompted me to give it all up, because I guess I have a somewhat different attitude about the music business than most people. I just got sick of the personality conflicts and the overinflated egos. There are a few of us left who could get together and write a book and tell a whole lot of things about the music business that would surprise the public. For instance, it often gets to the point where money is the *only* thing, and people judge you as a musician by how much you make. Today everybody is making money, but the music is going downhill. There are things about today's music that I don't understand and don't care for.

Do you do anything at all in music now?

No, I don't even have a horn anymore. And I don't miss a thing about it. I like music, but I just don't care anything about modern music. Today the music business seems like a hash situation. It's the product of some producer or promoter and is based on his idea of how to make money. And the money is mainly made by people other than the performers. To me that's very sad. The player is the person who should make the money off his own playing. After the performer gets paid, these other birds should be paid a small percentage for what they do. The idea of some promoter making 50 to 70 percent off your playing is completely ridiculous to me.

Is this what drove you out of the business?

It was mainly the personalities of the so-called leaders. Being a leader these days is mostly a publicity job. Most of them have no idea what makes good music. Nine-tenths of what I hear these days is junk. What is it? Can you hum it? If you can't hum it, what have you got? If we'd got the money in our day like these guys do today, we wouldn't need to be on Social Security. We used to have lots of good singers like

Robert Goulet, Perry Como, and Bing Crosby. Those were singers. You hear a singer get up today, and he sounds like a cross between a woman and I don't know what else. Guys are running around with hair down to their waist, like this Alice Cooper. It's not music, it's a freak show. But it's the recording industry management that tells us what we should hear, and they are the guys making all the money.

Forgetting pop music for a minute, what would you like to see happen to jazz in the future?

I would like to see a revival of good jazz, and see jazz back in the hands of the musicians. I'd like to see support for good bands, big bands, good tunes, and plenty of solo work. Maybe we could get people to quit thinking about the financial end and start noticing the artistic end. You'd be surprised how many musicians get ripped off these days. They play a session, and when they come to pick up their money they find that the money and the master tapes are gone. Vanished. That's demoralizing and frustrating, and I would like to see things like that wiped out forever. Musicians should be compensated for their work, and they should have a decent environment in which to work. Maybe then we could get back to making decent music again. Good traditional jazzmen can find a little work as background men in studio recording sessions, but I don't know of very many who are fronting their own groups and making a decent living—maybe some occasional club dates, but that's about all.

Were conditions better in the past—for example, on the Ellington band?

No sir, not much. When I was with Ellington I was paid $70 per week—when I played. If I played one day I got one-seventh, but I still had to pay rent, buy food, and have my laundry done. That's a whole story in itself, and I won't get into that now. Ellington had a monstrous ego too. I don't know if he realized it, but that band was the musicians. Musicians didn't get paid any better for their efforts than they do now. When we made records we were paid for the session only, and that was all. Once I figured out that I had made close to a thousand records, and if I had gotten royalties I sure would have no worries today. When I was with the big bands we would record fifteen or twenty versions of the same piece. Then we went with the small groups and made other versions, but we only got paid for each session—no royalties.

Let's go back to the start of your career. How did you happen to develop as you did?

After trying my hand at a number of instruments as a teenager, I settled on the trombone, because tailgating was the thing to do. But I began to feel more and more that it was silly for a trombone player just to get a smeared sound with the slide. Bands used to ride in trucks for advertising purposes, and they would put the trombone in the back so he could work his slide. I would never ride a truck; I wouldn't even walk in a parade. I just didn't look at music like that. I kept asking, Why can't this instrument be played in a beautiful, more cultivated manner? And that's what I tried to do. I didn't pattern my playing after any particular person; I just used my own ideas.

Speaking of how a horn should be played, what do you think are the most important ingredients in a good jazz performance?

In any performance, the ability to feel is the most important thing. If you're playing jazz, you've got to be able to feel the elements of jazz. If you're playing in a symphony, you've got to be able to feel symphonically. If you're going to be a soloist, you've got to feel the qualities necessary for that. For me, this has just sort of come naturally. Perhaps it had something to do with my family being musical.

I also had a big advantage in going to school in California. We had big orchestras. We'd have a little dance band and play some jazz on the side, but we also had the chance to play in big orchestras patterned after symphonies. It was the best experience I could have had. But you still have to have what it takes within yourself. A lot of things have to combine to make a good musician, but mainly you must be able to feel what you want to play. I can't explain it—it comes from within. For instance, I used to make up a solo in my head before I even touched the horn. In my mind I could frame the solo to fit the horn. After I thought it all through, I'd sit down and play it. I could also do solo work strictly ad lib—play maybe fifty choruses without even thinking of what I was going to play.

One of the greatest in this regard was Billy Strayhorn. His talent and ability were never really appreciated by the public. Another man that relied a great deal on feelings was Johnny Hodges. He could do more with a melody than anybody else in the business. I remember we were playing for some soldiers at the Cow Palace in San Francisco during World War II, and the things he was playing were so beautiful he had the whole place in tears. We need more players like him.

I feel that music has to tell a story, and it has to be something that impresses you so you remember it—even can hum it. It should give others something to feel, personally.

We have been talking with older jazz musicians about whether creativity continues to grow with age, or tends to fall off. What do you think?

Oh yes. We all begin to fall off at a certain point. After sixty-five, you're dying . . . going downhill. How many sixty-five-year-old hundred-yard-dash men do you know? The brain is the last thing to go, but it's going downhill all the time too. Benny Carter is an exception; he's phenomenal. He's been in the music business for many and many a year, and he still has what it takes to stay in the upstairs echelon. But on the average, jazz musicians don't last that long.

In a business where so many people seem to die so young, what's your secret for longevity?

Well, I think the secret is temperance, but not complete sobriety. I don't condemn drinking and partying, but I believe in doing things in moderation.

Are you temperate for religious reasons?

No. I am not at all religious. My father was religious—actually kind of a religious fanatic. When I started playing with jazz groups my father was pretty upset. I remember him saying, "In ten days you'll be in jail." Back in those days that could have been true. But I was a pretty independent person. Everything I did was of my own volition. I didn't pattern myself after anybody in particular, so I didn't have any terrible habits—the same as now. I still don't drink or smoke or use anything. I just go along on my own. I don't believe you have to be as religious as my father was, if you just adhere to certain fundamental laws, or at least try to. I believe there are some good lessons in religion—live by the sword, die by the sword; be temperate at all times. Those laws are important to me. But I still contend that no man knows what happens after death, or ever will know. That's the way I feel about religion.

Tell us about your daily routine.

Well, I'm alone now. I've been married a couple of times, but it didn't work out, so I live by myself in an apartment that Nellie Lutcher owns here in Los Angeles. It's a fine little apartment house with six units. I feel safe and comfortable there. Nellie's apartment is beautiful, and she drives a big Cadillac. She still plays some, but she also does a lot of charity work and she's on the board of directors of Local 47 of the Musicians' Union.

I usually get up about 8 A.M. I go and have breakfast, and then either go back home or go down and spend some time at the Musicians' Union hall. I was on a recording board at the union for about five years, but then I had three serious operations. That's why I'm not working at all now—can't get around as fast as I used to. I had a hip replacement and had to pull out of the position on the recording board. But I was retirement age anyway.

What are the worst and best things about being over sixty-five?

Well, the worst thing about being over sixty-five is being over sixty-five, and as far as the best thing, I can't say that anything is good about being that old. I do think that by that age you have realized what is important in life, but by that time it's getting to be too late. After sixty-five you're dying . . . going downhill.

Do you think that it's possible for older jazz players to retire comfortably, or do most of them face financial difficulties?

I think a number of them might like to retire, but they are confronted with a shortage of finances. A hungry jazz musician doesn't do too well, and most of us are hungry. Every time you turn around they're taking up a collection to bury some poor musician or they're having a benefit for his widow. Either the guy didn't have the sense to save any money, or he just wasn't in a position to. If you make $100 a day and have to spend $40 for a room and $20 for a meal, how much are you going to be able to save? These are the conditions in this business even today.

In looking back over your life, has it been a good, satisfying life by and large?

The traveling and meeting people all over the world has been the most gratifying experience I've had. All that travel amounted to a great education—to Japan, South America, India, and Europe, and they were different every time I went back. I learned a lot, seeing all the changes that were taking place. I'd love to make a trip around the world one more time. All in all, I've had a great international education.

Actually, my greatest satisfaction as a musician didn't come with the Ellington band at all; it was the four and a half years I spent working in the CBS studios in New York. That required a period of adjustment. First I had to learn how to blend with the studio players. I had always been a soloist, and my sound didn't match well at first. It was a great job, though, after I solved that problem. No road work. Just play the schedule, go home, and take it easy. But it was too good to last. After a while the studio work began drying up. Nothing lasts forever, I guess.

Eddie Miller. Courtesy of Eddie Miller.

Chapter 12
Eddie Miller

Eddie Miller started life where a real jazzman should, in New Orleans, on June 23, 1911. Although his father was dead set on moral grounds against his son becoming a musician, Miller was just as determined that he wanted to play. When the *New Orleans Item* organized a newsboy band, he started selling papers just so he could participate. He had his heart set on playing saxophone, but the head newsboy who handed out the instruments (and was saving the saxophone for a friend) insisted that Eddie would have to take a clarinet because he was "too little to play a saxophone."

By the time Miller was fifteen he was playing alto sax and clarinet in a local speakeasy with the New Orleans Owls. He married the next year, and his first child, a boy, was born in 1928, when he was seventeen. Although his salary was supposedly $35 a week, he was actually paid only half of it; the club owners said that they owed him the other half. New York seemed a likelier source of income, and Miller borrowed the train fare from a cousin to get there.

After an initial period of free-lancing, during which he was befriended and employed by Red McKenzie, the leader of the Mound City Blue Blowers, Miller got the chance to go with Ben Pollack, whose band he had idolized for years. The Pollack organization combined jazz and a commercial appeal, and included a personnel that sounds like a jazz Hall of Fame—Jack and Charlie Teagarden, Ray Bauduc, Charlie Spivak, Glenn Miller, Benny Goodman, Bud Freeman, and Jimmy McPartland.

Miller started with Ben at $85 a week (a substantial paycheck for a nineteen-year-old during the Great Depression), but he was forced to change from alto to tenor, fortunately for both himself and future jazz devotees. In 1934 the Pollack band broke up, but most of the

sidemen decided to stay together and reorganize as a cooperative
organization. Since no one wanted to front the band (Gil Rodin was
the manager), they began a search for someone with poise, maturity,
and a presentable appearance who could sing and was willing to go
along with the big band Dixieland format that had evolved under Ben
Pollack. Bing Crosby's brother Bob was the man.

The Crosby years lasted only from 1935 until 1942, when Bob
joined the Marines, but during those seven years the band was one of
the best in the land. A review of the group's performance at the Hotel
New Yorker in *Metronome* magazine in 1936 described them as "not
only one of the swing greats of the country today, but one of the
smartest and neatest all-round performing units heard in a long, long
time" (Simon 1971:60). Eddie Miller was praised as "a man who's
absolutely the last word in tenor saxing—a grand swing stylist who
achieved such glorious results because he seems to know just what he's
doing all the time, with the resultant splendidly patterned passages;
because he's such a master of his instrument he's a man who is
fortunate enough to be able to convey all the grand stuff he feels"
(Ibid.).

With Crosby's departure for the armed services, the band, still
democratic, elected Eddie Miller the new leader, but in 1943 he also
joined the army. He was discharged in 1944, and he and a number of
other alumni of the band went to work for the 20th-Century-Fox
Studios. In the late forties and the fifties Miller recorded with Paul
Weston, worked on Bob Crosby's TV show, freelanced around Los
Angeles and Las Vegas (often with Nappy Lamare), and even made a
movie, *Pete Kelly's Blues*.

In 1960 Pete Fountain (a fan of Miller's since childhood) invited
Eddie to come back to New Orleans and work with his Dixieland
combo in his club on Bourbon Street. It was a steady gig through most
of the sixties and seventies, but Eddie often took time off to rejoin
members of the old Crosby band for special engagements, such as the
six-week Rainbow Grill engagement in New York City in 1966 and the
record date at Evergreen-Monmouth that followed. Eddie Miller returned to Los Angeles in the late seventies, and to this day maintains a
busy free-lance performing schedule. He plays at jazz festivals, tours
Europe and Japan, has made numerous small group recordings, and
sometimes appears with the World's Greatest Jazz Band.

In George T. Simon's book *Simon Says* (1971), Eddie Miller is
included in its Hall of Fame as one of traditional jazz's best all-around
tenormen, able to play "gutbucket hot . . . commercial hot; he can
swing at a slow tempo; he can swing at a fast tempo. Besides all that, he
plays in exquisite taste with a grand tone. And he never kills that tone

to create an effect; instead he creates many of his effects by some subtle intonations. . . . For constant beauty I can't think of many musicians who have worn as well as Eddie Miller. I heard him a couple of years ago in New York, and the sound and style were as pure and gorgeous as ever" (1971:434–35).

What are you doing professionally these days?

I'm doing anything I feel like doing. I guess most jazz musicians strive to be able to take the jobs they like and turn down the ones they don't. I just returned from New York, where I went to do a tribute to Hoagy Carmichael at Carnegie Hall. The way the promoters talked, I thought I would be playing with the World's Greatest Jazz Band— that's the Yank Lawson-Bob Haggart group—but actually it was just a select group of traditional jazz people. We had Billy Butterfield, Yank Lawson, and Vic Dickerson. Bobby Rosengarten was on drums, Bob Haggart was on bass, and Dave McKenna was on piano. Bob Wilber played clarinet, and I was on tenor. It was a good band, but the promoters didn't utilize it well. Mostly we played behind singers. The group itself didn't get to play but a couple of jazz numbers. The affair was a big success, but not much happened instrumentally.

Is the World's Greatest Jazz Band a group you like to work with?

Yes. I've been to Europe with them twice. We've worked quite a bit together. Of course, the band is made up of a lot of my old buddies.

Do you think that you are playing as well today as you did some thirty or forty years ago with the Crosby band?

I don't mean this in an egotistical, bragging way, but I think I'm playing a lot better, because I now feel freer. Part of this freedom comes from playing with a variety of people with various styles. I have been fortunate in being able to play with some good musicians and some good groups—for example, I was down in New Orleans with Pete Fountain for almost ten years. I originally planned to work with him for six months, but Pete is such a wonderful guy and his band was so good that I stayed longer than I should have. But good as that experience was, I had to seek something more challenging after a while. The problem was that we played the same tunes every night. And if we didn't play all the old traditional Dixie stuff, the customers would request them. So I left Pete and came out to California, and I have been having a ball. My life these days is just wonderful. I'm free to do anything I want to.

Do you practice every day?

No. I don't practice at all. I think the saxophone played alone sounds terrible. If you are a piano player it sounds nice to practice, but not the sax. When I have a gig coming up I get my horn and I find a good reed, but that's all.

Do you feel that it is more difficult to be creative and innovative after you get older?

No. As far as I am concerned, it's easier, because you are not as committed to a routine. When you're younger and really active professionally, you tend to become mechanical. You play the same tunes in much the same way night after night. When you're older, life is less routine. You can try more things. If you get an idea in your head, you're not afraid to attempt it, and a lot of creative stuff can come out. I also think that an older person can be more creative because he's not trying to please anyone but himself.

How much are you affected by the people you're playing with?

It's easier to be creative when you are playing with good people; it is also a challenge to play with people with a variety of styles. A lot of guys are still playing in an old two-beat style. Then there are guys who play modern jazz, and some that just play a good traditional jazz swing style. Creativity doesn't necessarily depend on your style—you can be creative within any style.

Are there any young players that you are particularly impressed by?

There is one—Scott Hamilton. He works around New York and is very popular. All of a sudden he's come up like crazy. He has been greatly influenced by Ben Webster. Of course, that's a good guy to listen to. When you're a kid starting out you have to have some idol, but eventually you've got to evolve a style of your own. Hamilton hasn't actually settled down yet to a style of his own, but he plays very, very well.

Speaking about styles, I imagine that you have influenced your share of tenor players.

I was honored to learn that Stan Getz thinks that I had an influence on his tone, and Lester Young also said I influenced him. That's really a compliment coming from guys like that. The man I idolized as a kid was Frankie Trumbauer. I think that he was one of the first guys to really play the saxophone well. Most other players in his day had what we used to call an Italian or nanny-goat style of vibrato. Trumbauer got a nice, smooth, pure sound, and that definitely influenced the way I tried to play the horn. He influenced a lot of guys—Johnny Hodges, for example.

I know that you're getting a good deal of work these days. Do you think that there is a new interest in traditional jazz?

I really do. But I don't mean traditional in the sense of Dixieland. There is a lot of interest in swing out here in California, and I think also in New York. And the younger kids are coming to concerts. Most of them have only known rock and roll; they've never been exposed to jazz before. They come to hear what we're doing, and to them it's new music. It's good to see them there and enjoying what they hear. When I was a kid there were only a few record companies—Decca, Columbia, Victor, and Okeh. They would have monthly jazz releases, and we would run out to the music store and go into a booth and listen. That's how we learned to appreciate jazz.

Do you play mostly with musicians your age, or are they usually younger?

Many of the guys I work with are my age, although some are younger. I work a lot with John Best, a great trumpet player who was with Artie Shaw and Glenn Miller. His group includes Nick Fatool, Ray Sherman, and Ray Leatherwood, one hell of a bass player. We work the San Diego Jazz Club a good deal.

When you play with younger musicians, are you a hero to them or a has-been?

No, most of them know my background, and I am treated very well. That is what makes me feel good. I don't know what they say behind my back, but they have all been very complimentary.

Do you think a jazz musician should ever retire?

Well, I'm not going to. As long as I'm physically able to play, I'll keep on doing it. I don't think a person ever has to get stale. I actually think you get more ideas and more inspiration as you grow older. There are too many things to learn for me to retire. I want to keep striving to improve. I not only play to please an audience and other musicians, I play to satisfy myself, and I'm a tough critic. To play the kind of horn I want requires constant attention and work.

What do you think are the most important ingredients in good jazz performance?

I think of a theme, along with the tune itself. I think in terms of pretty notes and intervals. I'm not a honker—I guess I'm more interested in melodic structure. I try to feel a song out so that I can get a nice melodic effect.

Do you plan out your solos in your mind before you play them?

No, I don't play that way. I just formulate the ideas as I come to the various parts of the tune. I like to get a kind of story picture within the tune itself. Of course, it's important to be able technically to play what you want to present, and that takes many years of hard work. The kids today are getting a much better music education than I ever did. I can't believe what some of those kids can do today when they come out of college.

Somebody said that kids today can play everything on the horn except a melody. Would you agree?

Well, the ones that survive learn that skill. They also develop a style. Unfortunately, there aren't many distinct styles any more. A few years back you could recognize most musicians on records by their style, but now it's very hard to do that. For some reason many of the younger players are not trying to develop a style of their own. They are satisfied to sound like the guy they idolize. I think the ones who are more successful in the long run will be those who do evolve their own individual style.

What is your daily schedule like?

Most of the time I go to bed about 11:30, and I get up early. I do a lot of walking, and I play golf. I'm a lot less active professionally than I used to be, although I still play a great deal. I kind of like to stay close to home, but I do a fair amount of traveling. I go to Odessa, Texas, every year for their jazz festival. It's a fun week. Last October I went to London and worked with the World's Greatest Jazz Band for a week in England and a week in Germany. After that I did a four-week tour of Europe on my own. The two weeks with the band were fun because someone else was making all the arrangements. When I headed out on my own it was a different matter—a different place each night, a different country every few days, language barriers, and different groups at each stop. You never were sure what any of them knew in the way of music. Most of the European musicians know American music and copy American jazz styles, but that's no way to see Europe, always on the run. Thank goodness I had my wife along with me. When I got home I was completely exhausted and my son, who is a doctor, immediately put me in the hospital to recuperate.

When you work these days, what kind of music do you like to play?

Mostly Dixieland and good standards—Rodgers and Hart and Gershwin tunes.

Is Dixieland challenging enough for you?

Not really. You play these tunes so many times it's hard to get anything new out of them. Dixieland has been good to me, though. Back in the old days guys used to be typed as two-beat or four-beat musicians. I guess I was a two-beat man. I remember one time I was rehearsing a radio show with Dinah Shore and Tony Martin, and Dinah didn't like how one part sounded. She turned to me instead of Victor Young, the director and arranger, and asked, "Eddie, should that be two-beat or four-beat?" The guys in the string section broke up.

It's pretty hard to come from New Orleans and not have some feeling for Dixieland, and almost every band I have played with was oriented that way. The Ben Pollack band played with a Dixieland feeling, and so did the Crosby group. We would buy a stock arrangement and then alter it to give it a Dixie sound. We would make sure that all the guys got to solo, and then on the final ensemble chorus Matty Matlock and I would play a clarient-tenor obbligato in octaves, and that gave the arrangement the Dixieland flavor.

Some people maintain that there is a difference between New Orleans jazz and Dixieland. Do you make that distinction?

No. I don't see any difference. The Original Dixieland Band took Dixieland to New York. But the New Orleans Rhythm Kings were a more modern sounding, more swinging band. Nobody talks much about their clarinetist, Leon Rappolo, but I think he was the greatest. He had the most beautiful tone I've ever heard. He used to come into a speakeasy where I was working and date one of the B-girls there. He was just a short little Italian guy, but he was my idol. I had a little four-piece group and I used to ask him to play, but he would always say no. Once in a while he would decide on his own to take out his horn and play, and it was great. He had a big sound all the way up and down the horn. Fazola was greatly influenced by him and came pretty close to sounding like him. Rappolo once said something to me that I have remembered all my life. Whenever he came in I would show off and try to impress him with how many notes I could play. One day he said to me, "Let me tell you something, kid; it's not how many notes you play but what notes you play that counts."

What are the best and the worst things about being your age?

I really don't think much about age at all. I don't worry about numbers. Some days I feel twenty-five and some days I feel my age, but it's no big deal. When I was down in New Orleans with Pete I met some of the guys I went to school with, and geez, did they look old. And they acted even older. When I asked them what they were doing, they said, "Well at our age there's lots of things you can't do any more." I think that is a lot of baloney. As long as I can keep a positive attitude, I don't think I'll age like some of these other guys. I also think music keeps me young. I think I'd age faster in some other kind of business. I also have hobbies. I like refinishing furniture, and I have a nice workshop over at my daughter's house. The main thing is keeping busy and doing something you like.

A lot of people in your business have died very young. To what do you attribute your longevity?

Positive thinking and optimism. My dad lived to be ninety-one, so I have heredity on my side, but I also try to think young. I also feel that my wife has been an important factor in keeping me alive and healthy. She's a good woman and a wonderful wife. We've been married for fifty-one years. I don't go to church every Sunday, but I'm a Catholic and I believe in the Man up there. I say my prayers every night, and I guess He has blessed me with a long and happy life.

Do a lot of musicians your age have adequate financial means, or do many have money problems?

I think that many of them have financial problems. Luckily, I invested some of my money. Those investments, along with Social Security and the money I make jobbing, allow us to live fairly comfortably. I am in a position where I wouldn't have to play at all. I did quite a bit of investing those ten years I was with Pete Fountain. Fortunately, I invested pretty wisely, and now I think I am above the average as far as the usual musician's financial situation goes.

If you could do it all over again, would you be a jazz musician?
I sure would.

Jess Stacy. Courtesy of Jess Stacy.

Chapter 13
Jess Stacy

In 1977 a solo piano album was released, titled *Stacy's Still Swinging*. At that time Stacy was seventy-three. Reviewing that record for *The Nation* the following year, Nat Hentoff described the Jess Stacy performance as one of "flowing, imaginative variations upon variations" and concluded that "very few pianists are able simultaneously to sound so full of ideas and tone colors while also seeming to float." This, wrote Hentoff, "is swinging grace, an unexpected reminder of how durable the jazz spirit can be" (1978:285).

Born in Cape Girardeau, Missouri, in 1904, Jess Stacy began playing piano at the age of twelve. By the time he was sixteen he was playing on Mississippi riverboats. Besides playing ragtime piano for evening excursions on the river, Stacy also played the ship's steam calliope, which necessitated wearing a raincoat and rain hat for protection from the steam and cinders issuing from the stack. He had to transpose most of the melodies into the key of C because that required playing fewer black keys; they were the ones that permitted a greater escape of steam from the keyboard. He even taped his fingers, but nothing completely protected him from burns. For this hazardous duty, he was paid an additional $5 a week. Some critics believe that Stacy's strength and dexterity on the keyboard are a direct result of the force it took to depress the keys on this steam contraption.

With a style mostly self-taught but with several years of riverboat experience, Jess decided in 1924 to take his talent to Chicago, where in the Prohibition era he found plenty of work. He soon found himself in such musical company as Bix Beiderbecke, Muggsy Spanier, Frank Teschemacher, Eddie Condon, and Pee Wee Russell. Occasionally he had the opportunity to work the Sunset Cafe with the Louis Armstrong band. He would also fill in for Earl Hines when

"Fatha" took a night off. Soon people began to comment on the great similarity in the styles of the two men. Stacy worked the speakeasys of Chicago for some ten years, often on the payroll of such notorious notables as Al Capone, Bugs Moran, and Machine-gun Jack Gurn. The bands he worked with are unfortunately less well remembered today: the Joe Kayser, Louie Panico, and Art Kassell bands in the late twenties, and in the early thirties the Earl Burnett and Maurie Stein orchestras. It was in Chicago, however, that Jess believes that he acquired his big band style, which he has described as one that "helped meld with the band—to be a part of it and help link each section together."

In 1934 Stacy, now a man of thirty, was playing in a Chicago bar known as The Subway because of its long, narrow floor plan when John Hammond heard him and persuaded Benny Goodman to hire him. Another Chicagoan, Gene Krupa, joined the band at the same time, which gave it a powerful and impressive rhythm section. Pianist Teddy Wilson performed on trio and quartet numbers, but Jess was the big-band mainstay until 1939, when he left for the Dixieland-oriented Bob Crosby orchestra. Jess Stacy's tenure with Goodman (a man he often found difficult to work for) should have catapulted him to stardom, but he never seemed to get the right break at the right time. Take, for example, the case of the three-minute (five-chorus) Carnegie Hall concert solo. In 1938 the Benny Goodman band gave the first jazz concert ever performed in Carnegie Hall. Such stars as Count Basie, Lester Young, Johnny Hodges, and Louis Armstrong were also featured in a brief history of American jazz. This was followed by what has been described as a long and somewhat tedious and noisy jam on "Honeysuckle Rose." The finale consisted of the Goodman band's *pièce de résistance,* "Sing, Sing, Sing," and it was during this number that something very special occurred. Goodman described what happened as follows:

> Jess had been playing his butt off all week, but especially that night. He was like the Yankee's Tommy Henrich—Old Reliable, though you might sometimes forget that he's there. I was listening to what Jess was doing behind my solo and I got the kind of feeling you get once in a while after years of playing under all sorts of conditions— something was happening, and if I gave Jess a shot he just might do something completely fantastic. (Avakian 1977)

Although the Goodman arrangement of "Sing, Sing, Sing" did not normally include a piano solo, at a certain moment Benny pointed at Jess, who took his cue and ran with it. George Avakian called it perhaps "the greatest piano improvisation ever recorded" *(Ibid.)*, and Whitney Balliett characterized the performance as an "airy, calm, circular improvisation that rose heedless into the noisy air" (1981:147). W. W. Nash remembers, "I was standing in the back of the hall when it started, and a magical stillness came down immediately over the audience. I recall thinking, 'This is certainly the finest thing that has happened tonight'" *(Ibid.: 148)*.

But this historic performance did little for Stacy's career, for no one but the Carnegie Hall audience got to hear it until thirteen years later, and by that time Jess was semiretired. The 1938 concert had been recorded on overlapping aluminum discs using a single microphone suspended from the ceiling of the hall. The discs were sent to the agency handling Goodman's weekly radio show and eventually given to Goodman as a souvenir. They were not discovered until 1951, when Benny's children found them in a closet in his Connecticut home. Had they been released in 1938, Jess Stacy might have become as famous as his clarinetist boss, but such a break was not in the cards.

But despite setbacks and delays, Jess kept working; he was with Bob Crosby for three years (1939–41), returned to the Goodman band for a short stint, and then joined Tommy Dorsey for a year. In 1945 Stacy tried his hand as a leader. The band, which featured both himself and his first wife, Lee Wiley, managed to survive the lean postwar years until 1950. By that time things were getting tough in the music business, and Jess gladly settled down in California, playing a few small piano bars as a single and cutting an occasional record. In 1951 he recorded with Ralph Sutton, and in the mid-1950s did *A Tribute to Benny Goodman*. Somewhat discouraged by what was happening to jazz in America, Jess ultimately took an office job with the Max Factor Company, a position he held until retirement at seventy.

Jess Stacy now spends most of his time practicing (just for fun) on his new imported Japanese piano, working in his garden, and playing an occasional gig. He cut two solo piano albums in the 1970s, has appeared at memorial concerts, and recently appeared on the Marian McPartland program on the Public Broadcasting System. In describing the present Jess Stacy style, Barry Ulanov holds that it is a "curious mixture of Mozartian elegance and honky-tonk brashness. The trumpet-like phrasing comes from Hines . . . , the sweet, simple and beautifully melodic variations from Stacy himself" (1972:228). And George Avakian, in the album notes for *Stacy's Still Swinging* (1977), describes Jess as a musician with "razor-sharp time, errorless fingers and a musical sense and spirit that have grown through time."

How active are you in the music business today?

Oh, not too much anymore. I make a record every now and then;
I did one in 1974. I went back and played the Newport Jazz Festival
that same year, and in 1977 I went back to New York City and made a
solo album. Actually, I retired from the music business in about 1960,
when I went to work for Max Factor. I worked for them for six years.
I do play a few things now and then, however. And you might say I
am meeting new challenges all the time. When Hank O'Neal asked me
to do the solo album, *Stacy's Still Swinging,* he wanted me to do it
without a rhythm section, and up to that time I had never cut an
album without one. I didn't know if I could even do it. Anyway, they
suggested that I come by myself; maybe they couldn't afford to hire
two other people. But you know how it is these days. Unless a record
company can sell a million copies, they are pretty careful about their
investments. But I took a chance and said I'll do it, and I think it
turned out real good.

*You say that you don't perform quite as much as you did. Do you feel that
you have lost anything of your former ability, or do you feel that you are still
improving?*

I think I'm improving. If you play too much, if you play too
constantly, things just get old hat. You get stale in what you are doing.
But if you lay off for a while, things become fresher. Now take my
situation. I was playing in piano bars when I first came out here to
California, and it got so I played the same old thing all the time. I just
couldn't get away from it. I really came up with better ideas after I
had laid off for about six years. When I started playing again I sat
down at the piano and had more chord progression ideas than I had
previously. My thinking was better; my sounds were more beautiful.
At least that's the way it sounded to me. Even now I practice every day.
I did three hours this morning. I just got a new piano, a Kawai. It's
made in Japan. For the money, its good. It's a console. But I practice
all the time. Not music so much—just exercises. You have to, because
when you get older what you have going for you can disappear pretty
fast if you don't work to maintain it. And timing can go too.

*Some older musicians believe that once you get to be sixty-five you can't do
anything creative any more—that it is all downhill from then on. What do you
think?*

I don't think so. No. I think you can play a tune too many times,
so it sounds like you're reading it, and your playing gets stereotyped.
The other night I caught Benny Goodman from Wolf Trap, and it

seems like he is still playing some of the same old stuff. Stuff like "Silk Shiny Stockings." The same old tunes. I would imagine he'd get sick of playing those tunes over and over again.

What are the most important ingredients in a good jazz performance?

In piano playing, I like a balance of hands. I like to have my left hand going and my right hand going. I don't like what these kids are doing today. It sounds like they are all right-handed and don't even have a left hand. They play mostly right-hand runs. I don't hear much melody; all I hear is a whole bunch of fast notes. They can do it all, but they have no style—at least that's the way it sounds to me. They play a gang of notes, but not much music. They talk about playing "free form" jazz. That's where one person can play in one key and another in another key and they can bring it all together, and they think it fits. Now some of the young players are very well educated. They know harmony. They are Juilliard graduates, but I can't figure any style out of what they are playing.

Where are today's musicians going to acquire a style from? Do you think it was easier to acquire a style when you were coming up?

Oh, I think so. When I came up in this business I came up playing by ear. I am a more or less self-taught musician. I used to listen to the riverboat bands on the Mississippi, and I occasionally had an opportunity to hear Louis Armstrong, Baby Dodds and his brother Johnny, and one time Bix Beiderbecke even came aboard the riverboat on which I was playing, and I heard him play piano. He had a marvelous style of harmony, like in his composition, "In a Mist." I heard all those people, and they all had styles. I picked up a little here and a little there, but ultimately I evolved a style of my own.

When did you start playing professionally?

I guess when I was going to high school. We had a little group that played college dances. We often went to neighboring towns and played one-nighters here and there just to pick up a little money. The name of the group was the Agony Four. We used to listen to records and try to sound like some of the people we heard. Now we are talking about 1918, '19, and '20. We used to like people like Jelly Roll Morton. He was a big man on Victor in those days. For a while I worked in a music store—mostly sweeping out, but I did the sweeping to the music of the Original Dixieland Jazz Band, which was popular in those days. I heard all these people playing, and I would try playing by ear. I would try this and I would try that, but I really wanted to learn to read, because some of the artists had made stock arrangements, but they were mostly too hard for me. I could play the chorus O.K., but some of the intros and endings were pretty tricky. But I taught myself to read a little bit, and back in those days there were some pretty good piano teachers, and so I took a few lessons. That was never very successful, though. I guess I just couldn't meet their expectations of legitimate piano technique. I remember they were always knocking my hands off the keys because I didn't hold my wrists right. They wanted a concert style, and I guess I had a saloon style, I finally gave up on the formal lessons, but I kept playing. I started playing arpeggios the way I could and not the way they said I should. I sort of figured it all out myself. I was self-taught, and I am still teaching myself every day. When you're like me, you just never give up. Playing piano is a little like dope—once you start, you're hooked. I go through the same thing now that I did then. Practice, practice, practice. Up and down scales. Scales with both hands. Scales in octaves. You have got to do it, just to keep everything working together.

Has aging brought any special problems, such as arthritis in your hands or loss of hearing or eyesight?

No, I have no problems with my hands and no hearing loss other than what naturally comes with growing older. Nothing that hurts my music. Of course, I don't see as well as I used to, but it's no problem. My wife claims that I have some hearing loss, but I have a hunch it's more a matter of my not always paying attention. A lot of small talk isn't worth listening to anyway. Not wanting to answer and being deaf are two very different things.

Do you try to keep up with any of the newer ideas in jazz?

No, I just try to keep both hands going. I try to keep the same ability in the left that I do in the right. I don't really want to play like these young guys. I just want to keep moving along. I just want to keep what I have got and maybe develop the quality of it a little.

Are there any younger musicians today that you think are particularly good?

This is probably bad, but I haven't been listening a lot to some of the newer people. I do buy a few records now and then. I kind of like Bill Evans. I have quite a few things by him. But I don't really follow some of these modern people. There is someone named Cecil Taylor that plays free form, but I don't know much about his work. I do like Ralph Sutton and Dave McKenna.

Most of the newer guys have to have a rhythm section; they're just lost without it. I don't mind playing without a rhythm section because I can furnish my own beat; I keep the left hand providing the beat. And I insist on a strict tempo. But I don't think most of the younger players are capable of that. I don't like this free-form business. For me it doesn't all come together like it's supposed to. I admire some of these people for their technique. They are all over the blasted piano. But you don't have to be far out or avant-garde to be creative. The tempos they play these days are fantastic—I wonder who introduced these fast tempos. It occurred to me that some of this got started with the Goodman quartet or trio. Teddy Wilson could play at tempos that were just unbelievable. But the problem for me is that at that tempo things just don't swing. I mean they just downright don't swing. When stuff swings, it is just nice and quiet and just flows nicely.

We know that you have a reputation for being a great rhythm section man, but tell us about the circumstances surrounding that famous solo of yours at the 1938 Carnegie Hall concert.

Of course, you realize that I was not in the Goodman band as a soloist. Benny hired me to play time. But round about then, just before the 1938 Carnegie concert, I think that Goodman was getting a bit burned up at all the acclaim the jazz fans were giving Teddy Wilson, Harry James, and Lionel Hampton, and I think he might have been wanting to divert a litle attention from them. Perhaps he thought they were overshadowing him to a certain extent. Anyway, before I went on stage I'd had four scotch and sodas, and I was flying high through most of the concert. While we were playing the "Sing, Sing, Sing" number Benny seemed to like what I was doing behind his solo, and with no warning at all he turned to me when he ended his chorus and said, "Take it, Jess." I am glad I didn't know the solo was coming up, or I would have been scared to death. And if I had tried to rehearse that solo I would have fouled it up. As it happened, it all came very natural and I really felt good about what I was playing. Some say that that solo was very different from what I usually played. Some even say they see influences of MacDowell, Debussy, or Ravel in what I did. Well, my career as a piano soloist with Goodman was pretty short, but I guess I did attract some attention.

How do you explain your good health and longevity in a profession in which so many died very young?

Good genes, I guess. Both my mother and dad lived to be about eighty-nine years old. It's important to choose the right parents. When I was young I wasn't always too smart about the way I lived. I did a bit of heavy drinking and a lot of smoking. But I quit smoking in 1951, and I don't drink any more now. I also get a fair amount of exercise. My wife and I take little walks in the morning, and I do a lot of work in the yard. All this keeps me moving pretty good. It was about in 1950 that I started changing my lifestyle. All of a sudden I began to feel the pangs, the warnings. I started finding myself burning holes in the piano and I began to start feeling droopy, and I'd think I needed to get a cigarette. I sort of lost my appetite. I was also slowing down in my mind. These days if I take a drink, I just have to go to bed. I sure can't play worth a darn. My hands start feeling fat on me.

Do you eat anything in particular, or avoid any special foods?

Oh, sometimes my wife and I go on a diet to lose a little weight. I should take off about thirty pounds right now, but unfortunately I like to eat. But drinking is no longer a problem. I know that some of the young players have a drinking problem, but I think a lot of that is sheer boredom. The public makes certain demands on an artist, and about the only way you can survive is to do a fair amount of drinking. It got that way with me. Sometimes in a club you can't even hear yourself play, and you have to drink in self-defense. Between the smoke and the noise, it's almost more than you can take.

Do you think of yourself as retired these days?

Yes, except that I try to keep myself ready in case somebody should call me and offer me something challenging. It seems that about every three or four years I will be sitting here minding my own business, and someone will call me from New York and ask me if I would like to play a concert, make another album, or work a club gig. Of course, I practice about two or three hours a day, so I'm always ready. I am technically retired, but at the same time I'm ready to play whenever someone thinks they want to hear me.

What's the best thing about being your age?

Well, I think the best thing is that by this time you have more or less found yourself. There is no striving to get ahead, no trying to do this or that. You just can sit back and say, "Well, here it is; I'll do the best I can." I just practice when I want to; I like that. I like my house. I like what I am doing. I like my wife. What more do you want? I don't want to go play in those snake pits anymore. Last Christmas a guy asked me to come to New York and play in the Village Vanguard, you know, that basement. Eddie Condon made a cute remark about the place. He said that the smells from the kitchen were so bad that the washroom attendants quit. That's the most beautiful thing that he ever said. Well anyway, I told the Vanguard guy, "What! Come back to that smoke-filled joint? No, I've had enough of that to last a lifetime."

And the worst thing?

Well, I'm past the stage of being girl-crazy. I don't want to go out all hours of the night, live it up and smoke tea. I'm just coasting along. I guess there isn't too much bad about being seventy-five. I'm on my way to Saturn, you know. Since I got a little bit older I guess I have mellowed, but I never was much of a ham in the first place. When I look around at what some of these people think they have to do it to make it in jazz, I am kind of surprised. Now I see that George Shearing is trying to sing. Things sure have changed. When I played my first jobs in bands, I was hired to keep time. You didn't have to sing or make arrangements to hold a job, you just played time. Goodman hired me to play time, and the time was there too. Today you have to be a one-man band. I think that TV has brought that on. In my day we just sat there quietly and played. You didn't have to tell jokes and be a comedian. You just played time, and made the band swing.

Are you happy with some of the things you have been doing lately?

I've been listening to that record that I made some time ago. I was listening to one or two of those old tunes, and I think I did a wonderful job on "Lover Man." They let me play it for about ten minutes and fifteen seconds. They just let me go. You have to think ahead, you know. It is simple but effective. Too much technique sometimes gets in the way of being creative.

What about your retirement? Are you financially comfortable, or do you, like some of the other older musicians, have to play every once in a while to bring in a little extra money?

I have made some fairly good investments and my wife works every day. The house is paid for. We are comfortable. But I think a lot of musicians couldn't retire if they wanted to. Leaders have a good chance to make money, but there is just no way to make it if you are a sideman. Goodman made it big, but his sidemen didn't. It doesn't take a lot of money to live in retirement, but it does take something. I'm not starving and I don't have to work, but I think that a lot of older jazz musicians do. I saved a little when I was playing regularly, but when I tried to have my own band, I lost it all. When I came out here and started playing piano bars as a single, I made more money than I had in the earlier days with the band. Just playing alone, I could make two or three bills a week. I set some of it aside for this house.

As a solo jazz pianist, do you have any pet peeves?

Oh, I guess the only pet peeves I've got are bad pianos and banjos. Holy mackerel, one group I played with had two of those mothers playing, Two of those bastards. What chance has a piano got when two banjos are whangin' away? I just put my hands in my pockets and said "That's it." But I gave up that kind of gig years ago. I had another challenge back in 1974, when I cut the album without a rhythm section. I had never done that before. But I thought the result was better than a lot of other records I've cut. I didn't have to put up with guys making trashy rim shots and banging on cymbals. When you are trying to do something and you get all covered up by that, it just cancels out anything you might want to do.

Many of the older jazz musicians we have interviewed talk about their religious commitment. Are you a religious man?

I am not religious at all. No, I don't go to church or anything like that. Here's my church—just sittin' here where I am enjoying life. My wife is eighteen years younger than me, and when we got married in 1953 we had a beautiful church wedding. I'd had two bad marriages before, so I can tell you I can really appreciate things now. I sit in the back yard and say to myself, "Isn't this wonderful!" I have more patience too. I would take a gig now and then if I could get with the right guys, but I don't want to work too hard. If you play a two-handed style like I do, you really have to work at it. And I don't like to work four or five hours straight anymore.

What is your daily routine?

I get up at six o'clock every morning. My wife and I take a three-mile walk to the top of the hill, and then we come back. After our morning walk my wife gets ready to go to work. She has been at the same job for about thirty years. It's not a hard job—she works for an investment firm. She gets home about two or three o'clock, and we sit around and look at television or relax in the back yard. But while she's at work I spend a lot of time at the piano and play my whole set of exercises. There are a lot of things I haven't mastered yet and probably never will, but I will go down with a full head of steam trying. I don't know what the hell I'm practicing for, but it makes me happy. Maybe I am practicing to stay young.

I also spend a lot of time during the day reading about astronomy. I have read about every book that I can get hold of. I spend a lot of time looking at the stars—I'm interested in the Einstein theory of relativity and all that. Astronomy may be my religion. But I do wonder if there is some long white dude up there who with His divine hands created everything. I certainly am curious about how it all started. It says in the Bible that God created all of this out of nothing. With divine hands He created heaven and earth. Saint Augustine said, "Who could understand this mystery or explain it to others?" But it sure has me going. I never was religious, but I know the difference between right and wrong. I figure that when I die, wherever I go it's OK with me.

Chapter 14
Recapitulation

Having met our twelve jazz greats and seen something of the way they live now, perhaps we've moved a step closer to answering the question we started with: Are they really getting better with age? They themselves seem to believe they are, and most of them are still striving to develop their talents even further. Walter Thomas contends that "I am three times the musician now that I was when I was young. I've discovered a lot of things. In order to comprehend more you must put into practice what you already know. You learn continually." Milt Hinton says that if he is less daring than he used to be, with a lifetime's experience behind him he's now more sure of himself, and he insists that his technique has actually improved. And according to Johnny Guarnieri, "Anyone who doesn't improve in thirty years ought to find other work. It's a matter of normal growth. It's not a physical thing, and age shouldn't have much to do with it."

Doc Cheatham told us that "the longer I play, the better I get," and in a *Down Beat* interview with Lee Jeske in 1981 Doc said, "I find I'm getting better all the time. That's why I like the Sunday afternoon gig at Sweet Basil—it gives me an opportunity to experiment" (1981:73).

Marshal Royal, who played lead alto for Count Basie for two decades, observes, "You ought to be more creative when you're older. You have more to draw on, and you know how to conserve energy. You may not be as daring, but you have the advantage of knowledge and experience." Eddie Miller believes it is easier to be creative when you are older because you're not committed to a routine. Performing steadily night after night tends to deaden one, resulting in mechanical playing. He feels that he is more creative now because he is playing to please himself, on jobs he has chosen. He believes he's both freer and much more musically advanced now than when he was young.

In this he resembles an artist in a different field, novelist Pearl Buck, who in a 1967 article in *Psychosomatics* maintained that as you "grow older you have time to think, and when your brain is keen, you have something to work with because your mind is not cluttered up with other duties. . . . You create and study out of pure joy . . . and you become a new person" (1967:31). She insists that instead of growing smaller as you grow older, the creative life expands—"more to experience, more to learn, more to know" *(Ibid.)*.

Another literary figure, Simone de Beauvoir, sees the rules of music as more constricting than those that govern a writer, and believes that for the musician, aging is a progress toward a freedom that writers enjoy from the very beginning. The greatest degree of creativity is possible only when a musician has a body of work behind him, which gives him the self-confidence necessary for high achievement.

Self-confidence in old age is difficult, however, to maintain in our society, which so heavily favors youth. The problem in America is summed up by Gregory Bateson:

> Man lives by propositions where truth depends upon his believing them. If he believes that the old are no good, weak, stubborn . . . then to a great extent that will become true of the old in the population where that is believed and the old themselves will believe it and will reinforce the general belief that that is so. (1950:52)

As Americans age, they tend to do less than they are capable of and become less adventurous than they might be because they underestimate the value of their experience and the wisdom that comes with it, and because they're fearful of being made to feel foolish for not "acting their age." This is an inhibition that jazz musicians, perhaps because as performers they're freer from conventional constraints on behavior, have for the most part escaped.

While some degree of creativity is within the grasp of everyone, we believe that our sample of elderly jazz musicians represents an exceptional group. Their love of their art has kept them alert, interested in the world around them, and eager to seek out new horizons for growth and development. They have all the resources conducive to creativity late in life: maturity, wisdom, and experience.

Ours is a culture that admires winners, but handicaps the competitors during their senior years. Elderly people who cannot adjust their goals to match this reality, who cannot find alternate sources of satisfaction or a meaningful place for themselves in the larger scheme of things, will have difficulty maintaining a positive attitude toward life. The personal and artistic success of our group of older jazz musicians undoubtedly owes a great deal to their ability to adapt to the realities of the aging process and the competitive system, while refusing to surrender an iota of faith in their capacity to continue growing as artists. In their art, they are eternally youthful; that is the most striking thing about them.

In a study of longevity in highly artistic people published in 1965, Elliott Jaques concluded that gifted artists a reach a critical point in their lives in their early forties, during which time a changeover from the fevered activity of youth generally takes place, a change to what he calls "sculpted creativity." These artists manage to achieve a kind of relaxation that permits them many more years of productivity.

This seems to have occurred in some in our sample of jazz greats, who find it possible to carry on a schedule nearly as rigorous as when they were young, except that their activities are now of their own choosing, and therefore less fatiguing. No longer would they submit to the enervating one-nighters or late hours in nightclubs. Milt Hinton noted that his calendar was full of things he could do with ease. "I couldn't make it with Maynard Ferguson or Woody Herman," he says. "To record in a studio for two hours, or play a festival or clinic, is very relaxing to me. There is no strain involved." And Marshal Royal, after twenty years on the road with Count Basie, now says, "I seldom travel anymore. I mostly do recording jobs and TV work. I play big band concerts and now and then I play private parties, but I am selective about these. I have been asked several times to get into the clinic [teaching] deal. Some people my age get into so many things, they're running from one thing to another almost like the one-nighters. I like to play when things will be enjoyable. Then it takes absolutely no effort at all to do it."

A 1982 review of an Eddie Miller record, *Street of Dreams*, describes the laid-back approach he has evolved in recent years. Kent Hazen writes in *Mississippi Rag*, "Miller gathers momentum as he rolls along, and the longer he rolls, the richer his improvisations become. In this quartet session Miller has all the time he needs to develop and resolve his ideas, and the results are impressive" (1982:9). What these older musicians bring to performance now is a spaciousness, an ease, a breadth of mastery that's like a recompense for slowing down—if indeed they do lose any of their momentum.

While none of our interviewees attributed their longevity to an ability to relax and avoid stress, some reserach conducted by *Mississippi Rag* in 1977 strongly suggests that this may be a factor for jazz musicians. The magazine investigated the age of death of one hundred and eighteen New Orleans jazz musicians and found that bass players were on the average the longest-lived (73.0 years) and trumpet players the shortest-lived (65.8), followed by trombonists (66.7), and drummers (67.1). The conclusions drawn from the data were that (1) New Orleans is a pretty healthy town for jazz musicians, and (2) support instrument musicians such as bass players may garner less glory, but they also experience less stress, and therefore are rewarded with longer lives. Trumpet players, trombonists, and drummers, on the other hand, are more often in the spotlight, get more attention, and therefore are perhaps more subject to stress (Van Vorst 1977).

While trumpet player Doc Cheatham is certainly in the spotlight, his positive attitude toward his art and his love of music seem more than adequate defense against the anguish of competitive stress. Michael Ullman quotes him in *Jazz Lives* as saying, "I never wanted to be a leader . . . I just want to go and play. Now everything's coming easy. The money's not coming, but I don't worry too much about that. Music's something where the music comes first. I'm enjoying what I'm doing. That's all that matters" (1980:26).

Many of those interviewed (such as Cheatham, Royal, and Barefield) maintain that after long careers as night owls, they have now become day people. Most too are physically active, even athletic, or have inaugurated programs of regular exercise. Eddie Miller, Walter Thomas, and Marshal Royal play golf, and Howard Rumsey golfs, sails, and flies his own plane for relaxation. Eddie Barefield is a weight lifter and a runner, and Doc Cheatham walks between ten and twenty miles a day after a huge breakfast of his own fixing.

Jess Stacy spends a good part of the day just playing piano for his own enjoyment, and confides, "Now I can sit back and be calm and really appreciate what I've got. I sit in the back yard and look at the garden and the birds and squirrels and say, 'Oh, isn't this wonderful.'" His other great interest, a recent one, is astronomy, and he maintains that "I read every book that I can get—Einstein's theory of relativity and all." Stacy is pleased with his life as a senior citizen. He doesn't worry about when he will play his next professional engagement, or whether or not he'll be asked to cut a new record. He says, "I'm not trying to get ahead—striving to do this or that. I just sit back, and here it is. I like what I am doing. I like my house. I like my wife. I practice my piano. What else do I want? Why would I want to go play in one of those snake pits any more?" And Marshal Royal says, "I just don't go for all that stompin' and jumpin' and rompin' any more. Most of my playing takes place in the daytime now. I like daytime."

Several years ago Mary Lou Williams became disillusioned with the politics and materialism in the music world. For three years she gave up playing altogether while she explored Catholic theology, wrote musical works for the church, and founded the Bel Canto Foundation, an organization to aid needy musicians. When she returned to playing, it was on her terms. She was artist-in-resident at Duke University, she conducted a student orchestra, played a major role in a program to get New York street kids interested in jazz and in playing musical instruments, and played a few select concerts and record dates.

Eddie Miller is a lot less active professionally now than he used to be, he says, although even so he still plays a great deal. He also has some sustaining interests apart from music: "I like refinishing furniture, and I have a nice workshop over at my daughter's house. The main thing is doing something you like. It's important to keep busy."

Andy Kirk's activities in music, although curtailed, continue to be fulfilling, and he is still in the public eye. He recently conducted a concert at Carnegie Hall and is frequently musical director at dance recitals in New York City. Two days a week he teaches Bible classes at his church, and he is well along with an autobiography, *Twenty Years on Wheels.* He still writes music; a New York jazz combo called Harlem One More Time is using a Kirk original as a theme song.

Accepting an inevitable decline in physical powers is a difficult but necessary part of maintaining a positive self-image as one grows older. This did not seem to be a problem with our older jazz greats. All seemed very realistic in the way they coped with the minor annoyances of the aging process, such as normal changes in energy level, vision, and hearing. Few appeared to be depressed by their age or physical condition. Eddie Miller felt that "As long as I can keep a positive attitude I don't think I'll age like some of these other guys [boyhood friends in New Orleans]. I also think music keeps me young." Nor does Doc Cheatham seem to have any great problem adjusting to senescence. He says, "I do find it a bit harder to get my chops up now that I am older. Now I have to practice every day. When I was young I never had to practice at all. But now I can't do that. If I don't practice every day, I have trouble. I only practice about fifteen or twenty minutes—just enough to keep my lip soft." Doc also worries a bit about his teeth, a major problem for all trumpet players. He had just come from the dentist when we interviewed him, but so far he says he has had little trouble. Marshal Royal feels as he has grown older he has learned "how to conserve energy so you don't waste it. There are a lot of kids that put out twice as much energy as it really takes to do the job."

Since improvisation is the very essence of jazz, and all jazz musicians maintain that a "good ear" is essential for that skill, we were interested in the problems that might accompany the natural hearing loss associated with age. None of our group, however, was plagued by hearing problems. Most of them play middle-register instruments—trumpet, saxophone, or trombone—and this is perhaps the hearing range that holds up best. Red Norvo, the vibraharpist, we were told, must wear a hearing aid to carry on conversations but does not turn it on when he performs. The most interesting response was that of Mary Lou Williams, who said, "I don't have to hear it with my ears. I hear it in my mind." Mary Lou Williams is known to have perfect pitch, and she is so familiar with harmonics and the chord changes on most standard jazz tunes that she probably doesn't need to hear them with the external ear, so to speak. Milt Hinton suspected that perhaps he had experienced normal hearing loss but maintained he had no problems professionally because he thinks of the chords he plays as numbers.

While Eddie Barefield knows he was "a lot quicker and more technically proficient on my horn" when he was younger, "now I am a lot more knowledgeable about music." Johnny Guarnieri feels fortunate that he is a piano player. "If I were a trumpet player or a clarinet player, where I had to depend on my lungs or my lips," he says, "it might be more difficult to cope with being older." Milt Hinton is coping well. "I'm still comfortable physically about the bass—I can get around it just as well as I used to. My technique has improved," he says, and he enjoys playing "more than ever."

Some musicians, like Doc Cheatham, find jazz performance an elixir of life in spite of its enervating consequences. Whitney Balliett describes Cheatham in *Night Creature* (1981): "This inexhaustible player never falters. He plays and plays, solo after solo, evening after evening, and each time he is fresh and affecting" (1981:206). And in Greenwich Village, where until her death in 1984 Alberta Hunter was packing them in at The Cookery, she told a reporter who wondered about her hectic performing pace at age eighty-two, "Tired? Why, I'm enjoying every minute of it."

A remarkable adjustment to physical disabilities was made by Walter "Foots" Thomas, who suffered a stroke in his late sixties. Finding that he could no longer play to his satisfaction, he turned to composition and to the music booking business, which proved a new source of satisfaction: "There was one thing I have that most agents don't have. I know music. I know what sounds good, and from working for so long in Cab Calloway's band I know the music business, and I am familiar with the country." Walter Thomas was also working on a duet book for saxophones, and an exercise book, continuing an interest that began over thirty-five years ago, when he devised the first method ever for teaching the art of improvisation. "I've eased off a little bit," he says. "I don't stay up late like I used to. I love my home now, and I don't work so hard. But I don't believe much in age."

The one casualty in our sample, at least in continuing performance, is Lawrence Brown, whose retirement after fifty years of extraordinary artistry appears to be mainly attributable to health problems. After a lifetime on the road with the Duke Ellington band, where he suffered almost constantly with back trouble, Brown has recently been plagued with a number of physical complaints requiring major surgery. This, together with unhappy developments in the music business—the dominance of rock and roll and a dog-eat-dog commercialism—has resulted in his disengagement. While Brown continues to spend time at the local union hall, where he occasionally serves on special committees, as far as playing is concerned he has hung up his horn. Brown is a retired jazz great who had had his career, and now wants a rest.

Jazz and Ageism

As a group, jazz musicians are a tolerant and easygoing lot, among whom there is less racial and religious bigotry than is found in any other segment of society. There also seems to be less discrimination based on age among them than in any other group. When good jazz musicians perform, their age is never a factor in their audiences' appreciation, nor in the respect of their younger colleagues. Doc Cheatham says of young musicians, "They seem to accept me and appreciate the things I do. Younger musicians look up to people like Eddie Barefield and Milt Hinton. They call Eddie 'the Daddy,' and they call Milt 'the Judge.'" To this Hinton adds, "Because I'm the old guy now they come to see me when they are in town. Eddie Gomez, Richard Davis, Ron Carter. It's not a matter of teaching them anything about bass. It's more like a rap session. I'll pass on anything I can." Marshal Royal says that he is often approached by directors of young rehearsal bands in Los Angeles, who ask him to come to their sessions and give their sax sections some pointers. (Rehearsal bands are groups that meet for rehearsal only, to enhance their skills.) The directors of these bands know that twenty years as musical director and lead alto player with Count Basie have made Royal an invaluable resource to draw upon for advice on how to phrase, blend, and execute. Royal jokingly adds that they like him to come because instead of having to pay $50 apiece for private lessons, the whole sax section gets a lesson for free. But Royal finds satisfaction in being still in such demand as a instructor of young musicians.

Eddie Miller remains one of Los Angeles' most respected musicians of any age. While Miller tends to play with a number of older musicians—John Best, Nick Fatool, Bobby Haggart, Nappie Lamare— he says that most of the young musicians "know my background, and I am treated very well. That is what makes me feel good. I don't know what they say behind my back, but they have all been very complimentary." Doc Cheatham's experience has been similar. "They seem to accept and appreciate the things I do most everywhere," he says. "Even teenagers seem enthusiastic. When they come out to hear us they often rave over what we do." In a 1981 interview in *Down Beat,* Doc told Lee Jeske, "I have a lot of trumpet players coming to me wanting to learn something, but I can't [teach now], because I'm going to rest and relax more" (1981:73).

Religion

Considering the reputation jazz musicians have for loose living, it is interesting to note how many of our interviewees express a deep religious commitment. Johnny Guarnieri attributes his longevity, his lifetime of happiness, and his talent to the "goodness of God," and Eddie Miller affirms his faith by insisting that God "has blessed me with a long and happy life." Miller ends each day with prayer. Mary Lou Williams was a very devout Catholic, who even had a priest for a personal manager. Some of her most recent compositions have been liturgical works, such as *St. Martin de Porres* and *Mary Lou's Mass.* Andy Kirk spends much of his leisure time teaching church school at his Jehovah's Witness place of worship, and Milt Hinton serves the congregation of the St. Albans Presbyterian Church as a deacon.

Several of the musicians are Christian Scientists. Howard Rumsey begins each day with a bit of relogous reading so that he can "get in tune mentally." Foots Thomas believed that Christian Science showed him how to live, and even "enhanced my musical abilities, because it taught me where my thoughts come from." Marshal Royal says that while he doesn't get to church too often, "he respects all religions" and believes that "any religion that can help a person is worthwhile."

Eddie Barefield, who was brought up in both the Methodist (his mother's) and the Baptist (his father's) traditions, began a serious study of religion on his own as an adult. He claims that about thirty years ago he "discovered Yoga and found a whole philosophy of life."

He adds, "I'm not talking about standing on your head and all that. I'm talking about the evolution of the spirit."

While none of these people are fanatic or narrow, to most of them religion is a strong positive force in their lives, and one that supplies direction and inspiration. Some even see it as the main source of their personal happiness and professional success.

Family

Cambor, Lisowitz, and Miller found in their sample of outstanding jazz performers that a satisfying, stable heterosexual relationship had been a major factor in the success and mental health of many of their respondents. In our sample, good marriages seem important to both longevity and continued creativity. When asked about financial and emotional security, our artists often mentioned strong marriages as responsible for both. Several said that "a good wife to maintain the home and manage the money" had been vital to their professional life, but the importance of a concerned and capable spouse extended far beyond economic matters. While some of our subjects had been divorced, most had surprisingly stable marriages. One very active jazz performer had been married to the same woman for nearly sixty years, and marriages of thirty or forty years were not uncommon.

Postscript

While the interviews and other material were being prepared for this volume, we chanced upon three reviews of performances that appeared in *Down Beat* magazine in 1975, 1976, and 1979. The group under review was that of Benny Goodman, who during the 1930s was universally hailed as the "King of Swing." While we did not interview this extraordinary musician, for reasons explained earlier, we believe that what was written about his performance as an aging jazz musician is particularly relevant to the issue of aging and creativity.

All the reviews were written by the same person, John McDonough, about concerts at the Ravinia Festival in Highland Park, Illinois. In 1975 McDonough wrote:

> Perhaps the most important thing to say is that although Goodman's performances appear on the surface to be basically the same in terms of material and musicians, the content of the playing is delightfully varied. Unlike many veterans of Goodman's star status,

the clarinetist has refused to fall into routine solo formulas. Such pieces as "Avalon," "Undecided," "I Want to Be Happy," "Sweet Georgia Brown," and other BG staples are still there but after the first chorus, all bets are off. Anything can happen, and when it does the excitement is unmistakable. . . . Even when cruising, there is a freshness of thought in the uncluttered construction of his lines. In this respect, Goodman seems to have grown considerably in the last decade. . . . There is a more firm overall direction to his playing, but not to the point of predictability. (1975:43–44)

And the following year, when Goodman, then sixty-four, had reached the age when most men begin to prepare for retirement, McDonough reported:

There aren't many musicians who after fifty years of recording can still be considered going strong artistically. Hines is one . . . Duke was. Basie is in his own orderly way. And so is Benny Goodman, the only charter member of the *Down Beat* poll winners who is still winning them . . . The capacity for surprise is constantly there. And the exceptional can always lie just beyond the next bar. Goodman has kept his integrity as an improvisor. (1976:33)

By 1979 one might expect that McDonough's review of Goodman at Ravinia would include comments on the toll the years were taking of this seasoned veteran, but such was not the case. He wrote:

Goodman's concerts are often among the most spontaneous jazz performances heard today. . . . Goodman was full of simple, powerful ideas that swung without mercy. . . . Throughout the performance Goodman played with exceptional fluency and feeling. . . . If this past summer is any indication, Goodman seems to be still at the top of his form and anxious to play. (1979:71–2)

Coda

Our investigation of aging and creativity among thirteen (if we include Benny Goodman) senior citizen jazz greats leads us to conclude that they *are* getting better with age. A lifetime of experience and an intense dedication to their art have resulted with the passing years in improved performance and an increasingly more imaginative and spontaneous conceptualization. In a profession in which death at an early age is common, these people have achieved remarkable longevity. They are among the fittest of their profession in mental health, artistic motivation, and capacity to adapt to the physical and cultural restrictions imposed on older people by age itself and by society. In general they approach jazz as a lifework worthy of total dedication; they speak of their art with something approaching reverence.

Their music is characterized by structure; they consider their solos mini-compositions, and they think of themselves as composers not merely interpreters of someone else's creations. Their musical interests are eclectic; by and large they like the classics, and are at least tolerant of new jazz trends and avant-garde artists.

Not only are these jazz greats capable of exceptional artistic creativity, but they are also meeting the demands of old age with skill and resourcefulness. They live moderately, working sensible hours, traveling only when it suits them, and looking after their health, which they regard as a commodity as valuable as their musical talent. They live in the present, with an eye on the future; they love both their music and their lifestyle. None expressed this better than eighty-one-year-old Andy Kirk, who concluded his interview with "Heaven is my home, but I'm not homesick."

Bibliography

Avakian, George. 1977. Album notes from *Stacy's Still Swinging*. New York, Chiaroscuro Records.

Balliett, Whitney. 1966. *Such Sweet Thunder*. Indianapolis: Bobbs-Merrill.

———. 1979. "Jazz: A Burning Desire." *The New Yorker* (February 5). 118–120.

———. 1981. *Night Creature*. New York: Oxford University Press.

Bateson, Gregory. 1950. "Cultural Ideas about Aging." In *Proceedings of a Conference Held August 7–10, 1950, at the University of California, Berkeley*. M. E. Jones (ed.). New York: Pacific Coast Committee on Old Age Research, Social Science Research Council.

Beauvoir, Simone de. 1972. *The Coming of Age*. New York: G. P. Putnam's Sons.

Bechet, Sidney. 1960. *Treat It Gentle*. New York: Hill and Wang.

Becker, Howard S. 1951. "The Professional Dance Musician and His Audience." *American Journal of Sociology* 57:136–144.

Bourne, Michael. 1977. "Benny Carter: His Majesty of Reeds." *Down Beat* (February, 24:20–21, 50).

Buck, Pearl S. 1967. "Creativity and the Aging American." *Psychosomatics* 8 (July–Aug.: 28–32).

Butler, Robert N. 1967. "The Destiny of Creativity in Later Life: Studies of Creative People and the Creative Process." In *Psychodynamic Studies on Aging: Creativity, Reminiscing and Dying*. Sidney Levin and Ralph J. Kahana (eds.). New York: International University Press.

Cambor, C. Glenn, Gerald M. Lisowitz, and Miles D. Miller. 1962. "Creative Jazz Musicians." *Psychiatry* 25 (1):1–15.

Clark, Margaret, and Barbara Anderson. 1967. *Culture and Aging*. Springfield: Charles C. Thomas.

Cranberg, Lawrence. 1975. Communication in "Letters" column. *Physics Today* (July:11).

Dennis, Wayne. 1966. "Creative Productivity Between the Ages of 20 and 80 Years." *Journal of Gerontology* 21:1–8.

Easton, Carol. 1973. *Straight Ahead.* New York: Morrow.

Ellington, Mercer. 1978. *Duke Ellington in Person: An Intimate Memoir.* Boston: Houghton Mifflin.

Feather, Leonard. 1966. *The Encyclopedia of Jazz in the Sixties.* New York: Bonanza.

———. 1966a. "Howard Rumsey—Success by the Beach." *International Musician* (June:6, 29).

———. 1981. "Jazz Composer Made Real Impact." *Wichita Eagle-Beacon* (June, 5:19D).

Guilford, J. P. 1977. *Way Beyond the IQ.* Buffalo: Creative Education Foundation.

Hazen, Kent. 1982. Record review of Eddie Miller/Johnny Varro: *Street of Dreams,* in *The Mississippi Rag* (October:9).

Hentoff, Nat. 1978. "Indigenous Music." *The Nation* (March, 11:284–85).

Jaques, Elliott. 1965. "Death and Mid-life Crisis." *International Journal of Psychoanalysis* 46:502–14.

Jarvik, L. F. 1973. *Intellectual Functioning in Adults.* New York: Springer.

Jeske, Lee. 1981. "Doc Cheatham, ℞ for the Blues." *Down Beat* (December, 25–27, 73).

Klee, Joe H. 1978. Review of Benny Carter 4: Montreux '77 (Pablo 2308 204). *The Mississippi Rag* (February:13).

———. 1979. Record review of Mary Lou Williams's "My Mother Pinned a Rose on Me." *The Mississippi Rag* (April:16).

Lehmen, Harvey. 1953. *Age and Achievement.* Princeton: Princeton University Press.

Lorge, Irving, and L. S. Hollingworth. 1936. "Adult Status of Highly Intelligent Children." *Journal of Genetic Psychology* 49:215–26.

Lorge, Irving, H. Y. McClusky, G. E. Jensen, and W. C. Hollenbeck. 1963. *Adult Education: Theory and Method.* Washington, D.C.: Adult Education Association of the U.S.A.

Maduro, Renaldo. 1974. "Artistic Creativity and Aging in India." *International Journal of Aging and Human Development* 5:303–329.

Mainliner Staff. 1977. "Creativity." *Mainliner* (July:25–31).

Maslow, A. H. 1954. *Motivation and Personality.* New York: Harper and Brothers.

McDonough, John. 1975. Review of Benny Goodman Ravinia Festival Concert, Highland Park, Illinois. *Down Beat* (November 6:43–44).

———. 1976. Review of Benny Goodman Ravinia Festival Concert, Highland Park, Illinois. *Down Beat* (November 4:33).

———. 1979. Review of Benny Goodman Concert, Ravinia Park, Highland Park, Illinois. *Down Beat* (November: 71–72).

McLeish, John Alexander. 1976. *The Ulyssean Adult: Creativity in the Middle and Later Years*. New York: McGraw-Hill Ryerson.

Mead, Margaret. 1967. "Ethnological Aspects of Aging." *Psychosomatics* 8 (July–Aug.:33–37).

Merriam, Alan, and Ray Mack. 1959–60. "The Jazz Community." *Social Forces* 38:211–222.

Metronome staff. 1936. "Eddie Miller." *Metronome* (July 1936; reprinted in George Simon's *Simon Says*, pp. 434–35).

Nanry, Charles. 1979. *The Jazz Text*. New York: Van Nostrand.

Panassié, Hughes. 1934. *Hot Jazz*. New York: M. Witmark & Sons.

Placksin, Sally. 1982. *American Women in Jazz*. New York: Seaview Books.

Shapiro, Nat, and Nat Hentoff. 1955. *Hear Me Talkin' To Ya*. New York: Holt, Rinehart & Winston.

Shaw, Arnold. 1971. *The Street That Never Slept*. New York: Coward, McCann & Geoghegan.

Shoemaker, Bill. 1983. Record review of Doc Cheatham and Sammy Price's *Black Beauty*. *Down Beat* (June, 28–29).

Simon, George. 1941. "Stan Kenton Band Draws Raves." *Metronome* (November; reprinted in George Simon's *Simon Says*, pp. 173–76).

———. 1971. *Simon Says: The Sights and Sounds of the Swing Era, 1935–1955*. New Rochelle: Arlington House.

Tennyson, Alfred. 1969. "Ulysses." In *The Poems of Tennyson*. Christopher Ricks (ed.) London: Longmans, 1969, pp. 560–66.

Torrance, E. Paul. 1963. *Education and the Creative Potential*. Minneapolis: University of Minnesota Press.

Tynan, John. 1958. "Howard Rumsey: Lighthouse Keeper." *Down Beat* (July, 10:15, 50).

Ulanov, Berry. 1972. *A History of Jazz in America*. New York: Da Capo Press.

Ullman, Michael. 1979. "Doc Cheatham." *The New Republic* (February 3:25–28).

———. 1980. *Jazz Lives*. Washington, D.C.: New Republic Books.

Van Vorst, Paige. 1977. "Some Musing on Longevity and Immortality." *The Mississippi Rag* (April:3).

Wechsler, David. 1958. *Measurement and Appraisal of Adult Intelligence*. Baltimore: Williams & Wilkins.

Westby, David. 1959–60. "The Career Experience of the Symphony Musician." *Social Forces* 38:223–230.